Executive Transitions

Executive Transitions

Second Edition

DARYL FISCHER AND LAURA B. ROBERTS

ROWMAN & LITTLEFIELD
Lanham • Boulder • New York • London

Published by Rowman & Littlefield
A wholly owned subsidiary of The Rowman & Littlefield Publishing Group, Inc.
4501 Forbes Boulevard, Suite 200, Lanham, Maryland 20706
www.rowman.com

Unit A, Whitacre Mews, 26-34 Stannary Street, London SE11 4AB

British Library Cataloguing in Publication Information Available

Library of Congress Cataloging-in-Publication Data

Names: Fischer, Daryl K., author. | Roberts, Laura B.
Title: Executive transitions / Daryl Fischer and Laura B. Roberts.
Description: Second Edition. | Lanham : Rowman & Littlefield, [2018] |
  Series: Templates for museum trustees | Revised edition of Executive
  transitions, c2003.
Identifiers: LCCN 2017055173 (print) | LCCN 2018000313 (ebook) | ISBN
  9781538108406 (electronic) | ISBN 9781538108390 (pbk. : alk. paper)
Subjects: LCSH: Trusts and trustees. | Leadership. | Nonprofit
  organizations—Management.
Classification: LCC HG4315 (ebook) | LCC HG4315 .F57 2018 (print) | DDC
  658.4/2—dc23
LC record available at https://lccn.loc.gov/2017055173

∞™ The paper used in this publication meets the minimum requirements of
American National Standard for Information Sciences—Permanence of Paper
for Printed Library Materials, ANSI/NISO Z39.48-1992.

Printed in the United States of America

Contents

Foreword

Thank you for your purchase of *Building Museum Boards*. Since its founding, the Museum Trustee Association (MTA) has communicated strategies and best practices to museums across the Americas. We are especially proud of this latest edition of our *Templates for Trustees* series, which digs deeper into trusteeship than ever before and provides the tools for an institution of any size to build, educate, and inspire a successful board.

Throughout the following pages are guidelines and best practices from industry leaders, both staff and volunteers. You will also find eleven customizable and automated templates to help you keep your board organized and focused on the key issues and challenges facing your museum today. MTA staff is available to you for support as you work your way through the software.

MTA is the network for informing, advising, and inspiring museum trustees. For more information on our products, publications, and services, visit us at www.museumtrustee.org or call our offices. We look forward to hearing from you!

Richard Kelly
Board Chairman
Museum Trustee Association

Mary Baily Wieler
President
Museum Trustee Association

About *Templates for Trustees*

"When it comes to board information," says Harvard University professor Richard Chait, "less is more, and much less is much more."[1] Trustees usually receive too much information with too little meaning. Instead, they need structured, concise materials that enhance board performance and satisfaction. Technology can direct trustees' attention to what matters most, helping them gather relevant information and explore it from different perspectives.

Templates for Trustees is a four-part series designed by the Museum Trustee Association (MTA) to focus attention on the processes and tasks of governance. It supports the MTA's mission "to enhance the effectiveness of museum trustees" by

- promoting and facilitating dialogue between museum trustees and museum directors
- collecting and disseminating information on museum governance that will assist trustees in discharging their responsibilities more effectively
- providing education and training opportunities for museum trustees
- initiating and conducting research on issues of concern to museum trustees

The templates are tools that present board information so that it can be collected, explored, and understood from different perspectives. Each one helps boards create documents, spreadsheets, and presentations tailored to their own needs. Using fill-in-the-blank forms, surveys, and rating scales that are provided on a unique cloud-based app, trustees or administrators enter specific information about their museum and their board. The completed templates and reports serve as starting points to help boards organize their thoughts, identify their priorities, and plan their actions.

Executive Transitions is the third publication in the four-part series. The other volumes include *Building Museum Boards* (volume 1), *The Leadership Partnership* (volume 2), and *Strategic Thinking and Planning* (volume 4). All books in the series are available on a web-based application that is accessible to both PC and Mac users.

All four volumes include five sections:

- **Using the *Templates for Trustees* Online App** provides an overview of how the website is structured and a brief description of the purpose and functionality of each template and report. Specific instructions for working with the document library and web-based forms and customizing the templates for each museum's needs are available on the website. This online **Help Manual** will be useful to the administrator, the staff, or the board member who will modify the forms so they are tailored to individual boards.

- The **User's Guide** suggests how to take full advantage of the text, templates, resources, and appendices. It also provides a brief overview of the entire search and transition process, which will be useful to everyone on the Search Committee.
- A summary of relevant issues and trends, **Transition as an Opportunity for Strategic Growth**, sets the stage for this work.
- **Chapters 1–4** discuss the process in detail and present examples of filled-in templates from hypothetical boards, which provide illustrations of how to interpret the information.
- The **Resource Guide** includes publications, job posting websites, and organizations with additional information on the executive search and transition process.

TERMINOLOGY

In these volumes we have used the following terms:

- *Template library* includes the complete set of tools: surveys, database forms, documents, calendars, and presentations.
- *Template* refers to any tool that is modified by the administrator and filled out by board members.
- *Reports* are generated by compiling the responses to completed templates.
- *Trustee* refers to a member of the museum's governing board. We use the terms *board member* and *trustee* interchangeably throughout this manual.
- *Director* is the staff leader who reports to the board. Some museums may use *executive director, chief executive officer (CEO),* or *president.*
- *Board chair* is the senior board member who oversees all board functions. Some boards may use *chief volunteer officer (CVO)* or *president.*
- *Interim leader* is the person who leads the staff and board between the departure of the previous director and the arrival of the new director.
- *Administrator* is the individual—typically a staff member in the executive office—who facilitates the search process and modifies and manages the templates.
- *Search Committee* is the group charged with identifying the most important qualities needed in a new leader and then recruiting, selecting, and orienting that person.
- *Personnel Committee* is the standing committee charged with determining staff salaries and benefits. For museums that do not have a Personnel Committee, the Executive Committee may serve this function.
- *Transition Task Force* is charged with facilitating the new director's transition. This board/staff team may include members of the Search Committee, Executive Committee, committee and task force chairs, and staff leaders.
- *Interim Leadership Teams* are groups of board and/or staff members who help to maintain momentum during the search process.

TEMPLATE SUPPORT

The Museum Trustee Association provides support to boards that purchase *Templates for Trustees.* Please contact the MTA at Support@MuseumTrusteeTemplates.org

- for more information or to order additional volumes in the series
- with questions about tailoring or troubleshooting your templates (service included in the one-time setup fee)

- if you would like to make a testimonial about your experience using this or other volumes in the *Templates for Trustees* series

NOTE

1. Chait made this observation during a panel on "The New Work of the Nonprofit Board" at the American Association of Museums Annual Meeting in Baltimore, Maryland, in April 2000.

Using the *Templates for Trustees* Online App

The physical book you are holding in your hands is just one part of *Executive Transitions*. The templates themselves, which can be tailored to your institution, are stored in an online application hosted by the Museum Trustee Association (MTA). To activate your account in the application, you will need to contact the MTA at support@ museumtrusteetemplates.org, pay a modest one-time setup fee (waived for MTA members), and schedule a time to set up your account. Once you create an account, you can begin to review and customize the eleven templates in *Executive Transitions*.

Throughout *Executive Transitions* and the other books in the series, there is an important role for the "administrator" who manages the museum's use of the online application. In a larger museum, there may be someone who already manages board communication as part of his or her job. In a smaller museum, the administrator may be the director or a board member. It is also possible for two people to share that role. Once you have identified the individual who will fill that role, he or she should set up the application.

INITIAL SETUP

Step one is registering your account with the Museum Trustee Association by sending an email to support@ museumtrusteetemplates.org. The MTA staff member responsible for administering *Templates for Trustees* will send the administrator a short version of your museum's name (Museum ID), the administrator's username, and a password, which will ensure the privacy and security of your museum's information. MTA staff will also schedule a telephone call to go through the rest of the setup process.

Step two is logging into the application at www.museumtrusteetemplates.org. The first screen (figure 0.1) is the *Templates for Trustees* landing page, with general information about the MTA.

From there, click "Log in" on the blue bar to continue. Enter the information provided by MTA (figure 0.2).

After logging in, you will be on the landing page for the four volumes in *Templates for Trustees* (figure 0.3).

Step three: Before setting up any single volume, the administrator should establish the global settings. This will enable the application to customize the templates (figure 0.4). Click on "Settings" to launch the page with the placeholder settings. For each item in Settings—the museum name, mission statement, director's name, the title used by the director, and the first month of the museum's fiscal year, annual meeting, or the start of the board cycle—click on "Edit" and put the appropriate information in the field labeled "Setting Value." Click "Save," and you will be returned to the list of Settings. *Note*: You will not see the changes immediately. Close this menu. Reopen "Settings," and you will see the changes.

FIGURE 0.1
MTA *Templates for Trustees* Home Page (Courtesy of the Museum Trustee Association)

FIGURE 0.2
MTA *Templates for Trustees* Log In (Courtesy of the Museum Trustee Association)

MUSEUM
TRUSTEE
ASSOCIATION

Log in

Museum Id

User name or email

Password

LOG IN   ☐ Remember me   Forgot password?

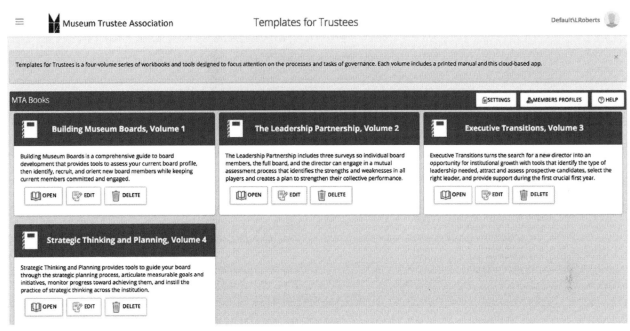

FIGURE 0.3
MTA *Templates for Trustees* Four Volumes Landing Page (Courtesy of the Museum Trustee Association)

For the Settings menu and most of the screenshots that follow, the information is for a fictitious museum—the Greenville Museum of Art and History—and its board.

Settings/Placeholders

Description	Value		
The title used by the director	Executive Director	EDIT	DELETE
The director's name	Jordan Charles	EDIT	DELETE
The museum's mission statement	Greenville Museum of Art and History broadens and deepens the community's connections to the heritage and culture of the region.	EDIT	DELETE
Month of the annual meeting and board elections	January	EDIT	DELETE
The name of the museum	Greenville Museum of Art and History	EDIT	DELETE

ADD

CLOSE

FIGURE 0.4
MTA *Templates for Trustees* Global Settings (Courtesy of the Museum Trustee Association)

Step four is creating a *Templates for Trustees* user account for everyone currently on the board, the director, and the administrator. Next to the MTA logo is a three-bar icon that opens the "Administration" menu (figure 0.5). Click that, and a new column will open on the left side with an arrow next to "Administration" (figure 0.6). Click on the arrow to open the menu and select "Users" (figure 0.7).

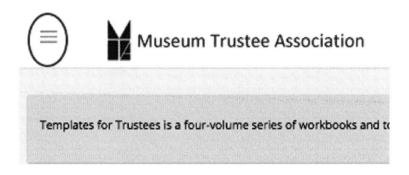

FIGURE 0.5
Executive Transitions Administration Menu
Opener (Courtesy of the Museum Trustee
Association)

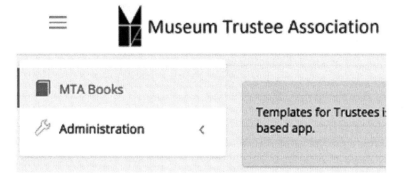

FIGURE 0.6
Executive Transitions Administration Menu
Selections (Courtesy of the Museum Trustee
Association)

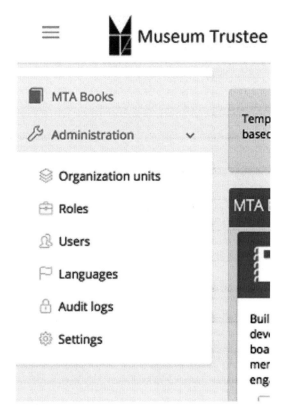

FIGURE 0.7
Executive Transitions Administration Menu Selector (Courtesy of
the Museum Trustee Association)

Click on the blue "Create New User" box (figure 0.8).

FIGURE 0.8
Executive Transitions New User Setup (Courtesy of the Museum Trustee Association)

A window will pop up (figure 0.9) where you can enter basic information for each member of the board: name, email address, and a username. We suggest deciding on a convention for creating usernames: *first initial last name* is common. Note that the system will automatically send the new user an email with instructions for choosing a personal password.

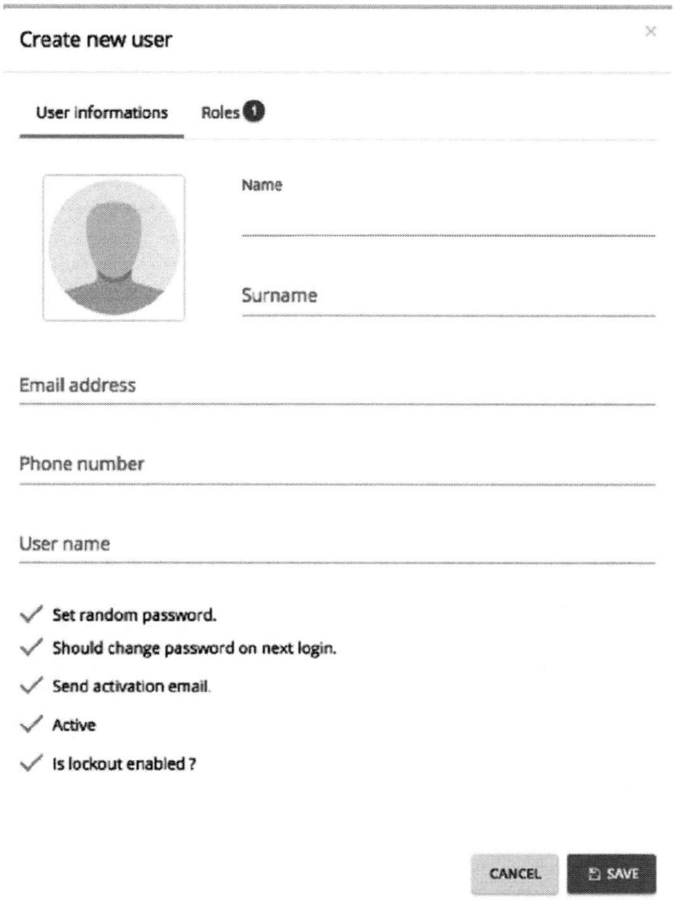

Create new user ×

User informations   Roles ①

Name

Surname

Email address

Phone number

FIGURE 0.9
Executive Transitions New User Activation (Courtesy of the Museum Trustee Association)

User name

✓ Set random password.
✓ Should change password on next login.
✓ Send activation email.
✓ Active
✓ Is lockout enabled ?

CANCEL   💾 SAVE

Every user has one or more "roles" that determine their access to various features. In general, the roles are members and chair of the relevant committee (for this template, the Search Committee), board members, Executive Committee members, board chair, executive director, and administrator. Just above the user's name, you will see "Roles" and a number in a blue circle. At first, that number will be "1" for the basic role of User. To add roles, click that circle. A menu of further roles opens; check all roles that user has and save (figure 0.10).

Because each of the roles will have different needs for information, there are different levels of access to templates and reports. Aside from the administrator, the chair of the Search Committee will have the most extensive access to the files in this volume. Members of the Search Committee will have greater access than other members of the board so that they can do the work of the committee. (Please note: Because this list of users is accessed by all of the *Templates for Trustees*, there are roles that are not relevant to *Executive Transitions*. The administrator can add those roles when setting up other volumes.)

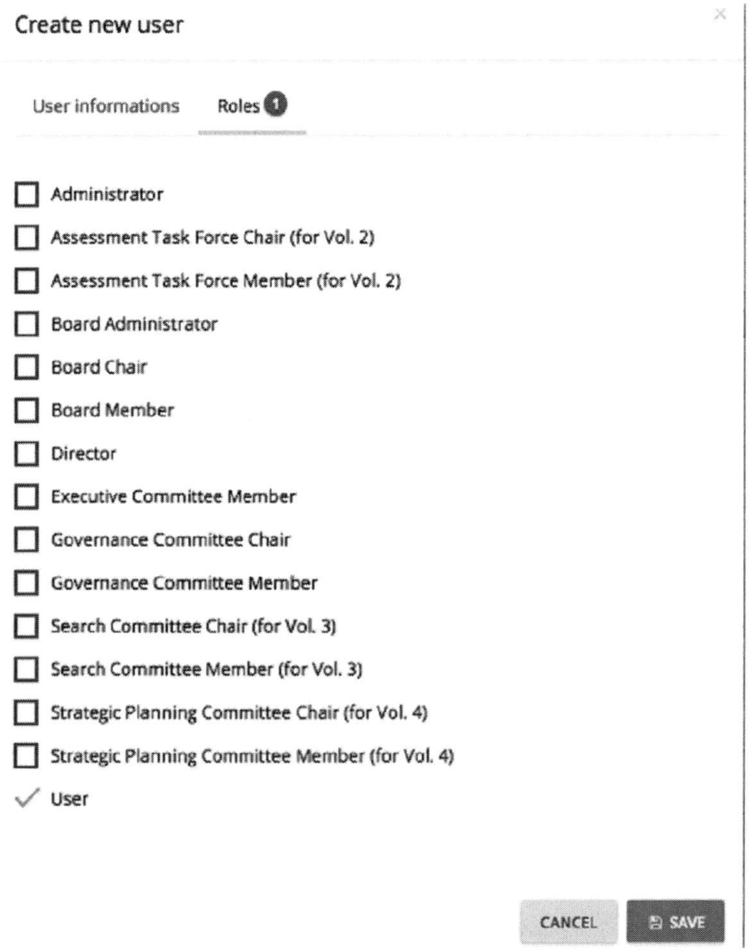

FIGURE 0.10
Executive Transitions User Roles (Courtesy of the Museum Trustee Association)

Create new user   ×

User informations   Roles ❶

☐ Administrator
☐ Assessment Task Force Chair (for Vol. 2)
☐ Assessment Task Force Member (for Vol. 2)
☐ Board Administrator
☐ Board Chair
☐ Board Member
☐ Director
☐ Executive Committee Member
☐ Governance Committee Chair
☐ Governance Committee Member
☐ Search Committee Chair (for Vol. 3)
☐ Search Committee Member (for Vol. 3)
☐ Strategic Planning Committee Chair (for Vol. 4)
☐ Strategic Planning Committee Member (for Vol. 4)
✓ User

                                                        CANCEL   💾 SAVE

All of the users are entered into a table for further customizing and editing (figure 0.11). Click the blue "Actions" button next to the user's name and select "Edit." There is also a button that allows the administrator to "Create New User," which brings up the same screen shown in figure 0.9.

FIGURE 0.11
Executive Transitions User Edits (Courtesy of the Museum Trustee Association)

Every user must have an email address associated with their user profile. If one or more board members do not use email, we suggest setting up an account on the museum's email system, with mail forwarded to the administrator. That way, whenever an email is generated for the board member(s), the administrator will receive the intended survey, report, form, or document and can print a hard copy to send to the board member(s) by mail or arrange for it to be picked up at the museum.

Step five: Having set up all of the museum's users, it is time to start using the templates. Return to the three-bar menu next to the MTA logo and select "MTA Books" (figure 0.12), which will bring you back to the landing page for the four volumes in *Templates for Trustees*. Having purchased *Executive Transitions*, that publication will be live.

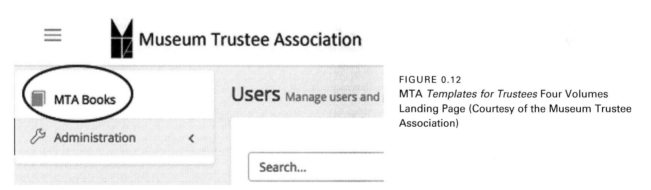

FIGURE 0.12
MTA *Templates for Trustees* Four Volumes Landing Page (Courtesy of the Museum Trustee Association)

In addition to these basic instructions, *Templates for Trustees* has an online Help function with more detailed and specific instructions. The "Help" button is always on the blue bar, next to "Settings" and "Members Profiles" (figure 0.13).

FIGURE 0.13
Templates for Trustees Help Button (Courtesy of the Museum Trustee Association)

Executive Transitions User's Guide

Many museum boards feel overwhelmed and under-resourced in their search for a new executive. This reaction is not surprising given that the search is added to their many other volunteer responsibilities. As public institutions, museums' stakeholders are often keenly interested in leadership transitions. Incorporating external perspectives is a valuable but time-consuming task for volunteers who are already stretched for time.

Unless they hire a search firm, boards have very little help in this critical task. Other aspects of board leadership have generated large bodies of literature, but not as much has been written about the executive search. This publication will be useful to both boards that hire a search firm and those that choose to conduct their own search. Users will range from small museums with just a few paid staff members who must pick up the responsibilities of the director to large museums with many staff members and transition budgets that allow them to hire interim leadership. Small museums may not be able to follow all the recommended steps and utilize all the templates, but this will still be a very useful framework as time and resources permit.

Whatever the size of your institution, we encourage you not to rule out suggestions that may seem beyond your reach. You may be able to draw on pro bono help or volunteers from other community organizations that have engaged in successful executive search processes. And whatever the cost of your search process, remember this: there is no more important investment the board can make in the future of any museum than finding the right leader.

We recommend that you approach this material in four steps:

1. Read this **User's Guide** for an overview of the entire process. It is a helpful summary of the entire search and transition process.
2. Read **Chapters 1–4,** which outline the search and transition process and introduce you to the templates and reports through examples that are incorporated in the text. You'll see the specific issues that are addressed and the formats in which they are presented.
3. **Using the Online App** is primarily written for the administrator who will be setting up and managing the application, although the Search Committee chair and others may also be interested in seeing how it functions. The administrator will also use the online **Help Manual** to learn how to tailor specific templates to your museum's search process. Any revisions should be made before sharing the link with the Search Committee and the rest of the board.
4. Consult the **Resource Guide** for helpful publications and websites for posting position announcements and the **Appendices** for suggestions of materials that will be useful to interim and new directors and assistance planning and facilitating Search Committee meetings.

Looking ahead, it helps to realize that there are four parts to a successful executive search process and four analogous chapters in this book.

Chapter 1: Preparing for a New Future: Being prepared for unforeseen events is among the board's most challenging roles and valuable contributions. Executive transitions begin when the tenure of the previous director ends. This often happens with very little advance warning, but when a director announces his or her intention to retire at some future date, there may be enough time for the search to be completed before the director leaves. Whatever the timeline, the process requires patience, persistence, and confidence. Since the search process follows a chronological, linear progression of steps, this book and the accompanying templates are organized in three stages: groundwork, search, and transition.

Chapter 2: The Groundwork Stage: This stage is the foundation for the rest of the search process. In a hurry to find a new leader, many institutions are tempted to skip this stage and jump right into the search. But building without a firm foundation can have disastrous consequences. To lay the groundwork, the board must first allocate the human and financial resources for the search. The board chair and the Executive Committee will then identify and recruit a Search Committee chair and members, sharing job descriptions that clarify the expectations for those charged with the important task of finding the museum's new leader. One of the Search Committee's first jobs is identifying the museum's current strengths and weaknesses. It will begin by conducting an Institutional Audit to gather necessary perspectives, and then holding a retreat with the Executive Committee or, in the case of small boards, the full board to envision the new director's greatest opportunities and challenges.

Chapter 3: The Search Stage: This stage involves most of the steps that boards identify with an executive search; it is important to underscore that this is the second stage in the process, not the first and not the last. Having completed the groundwork stage, the Search Committee identifies and prioritizes the professional skills and personal qualities most needed in the new director. Then it is ready to outline the duties and expectations for the position in a written job description and position announcement. After advertising in both print and electronic media and sourcing candidates through professional networks, the committee will evaluate the initial pool of applicants, conduct phone interviews with those on the short list, and identify and interview the top candidates. Reference checks on the finalists follow, after which the committee will make its recommendations to the full board. With board approval, the Search Committee chair will extend an offer to its top candidate.

Chapter 4: The Transition Stage: Even when there is an accepted offer, the committee's work is not done. To maximize the investment of time and energy that has been devoted to hiring the new director, it is important to plan for a smooth transition. The end of the search process signals the beginning of a new future for the museum. From the time the new director is hired to his or her first anniversary, the Search Committee, a transition task force, and the board will work together to plan the most effective orientation and introductions. They will schedule meetings, retreats, and assessments throughout the first year, using the Transition Calendar and consulting the books, periodicals, websites, and organizations listed in the **Resource Guide**. They will also work with the new director to establish measurable goals and objectives for his or her first year and monitor progress toward achieving them.

Acknowledgments

John Adkins's thirty years of experience with technology includes writing apps for Fortune 500 companies. His knowledge and experience helped move *Templates for Trustees* into the twenty-first century with the introduction of the online app that is an integral part of each volume in this series. We are grateful for his creativity and persistence, which met every challenge we encountered in implementing this new platform.

Executive Transitions reflects the combined experience and wisdom of countless individuals—paid staff members and volunteer board members—who have given us valuable feedback on both content and format. Their experiences are the best teachers. One of the great benefits of working and volunteering in museums is the spirit of collegiality that prevails and the generosity with which ideas and processes are shared.

In particular, we would like to thank David Ellis for sharing his wisdom and experience as interim director of the Harvard Museum of Natural History, interim president of the Boston Children's Museum, and search committee chair at the MIT Museum, as well as service on many searches and board governance committees.

Diane Frankel shared her many years of experience providing executive search services to a wide variety of arts and cultural organizations, both as an independent consultant and as an affiliate of Management Consultants for the Arts.

Maureen Robinson offered her perspective as facilitator of numerous leadership development workshops offered by the American Alliance of Museums.

The Museum Trustee Association and the authors thank Colleen Boland, coauthor of the first edition, and the dedicated group of advisors who contributed to that publication.

The Institute of Museum and Library Services, the primary source of federal support for the nation's museums and libraries, helped make possible the publication of the first edition of *Executive Transitions*.

The Museum Trustee Association gratefully acknowledges the following donors whose support made this series possible:

The Wieler Family Foundation in honor of Mary Baily Wieler and Emily Inglis
Georgina T. and Thomas A. Russo
Margaret and Bill Benjamin
Andrew L. and Gayle Shaw Camden
Richard and Mary Kelly
Maureen Pecht King
Janis and William Wetsman Foundation
Kristine and Leland Peterson
Katherine Duff Rines

Introduction

Transition as an Opportunity for Strategic Growth

The hiring of a new director is a major strategic event in the life of a museum. Whether the need for new leadership is brought about by a director's decision to resign or retire or a difficult board decision and whether it is received with feelings of loss or sighs of relief, it presents a tremendous opportunity for institutional growth. The retirement of a long-standing and much-loved director, a move dictated by a personal situation, an offer that was simply too good to pass up, or the dismissal of an ineffective leader—each situation brings different challenges for the board, staff, and volunteers that can stimulate renewed focus, energy, and commitment.

Ideally, the succession process is anticipated and planned for, as was the case at the Montshire Museum of Science in Norwich, Vermont. In 2013 the director informed the board of his intent to retire in two years. The board and staff seized the opportunity and used this time to full advantage, creating a new strategic vision for the museum, and then hiring a consultant who helped them find the best person to realize this vision.[1] This is certainly a model to which many boards aspire, but in reality, most find themselves with little time to fill leadership vacancies and with few plans to guide them. This is because leadership succession rarely rises to the top of a board's priority list until it becomes an urgent need. The authors of a recent article in *Nonprofit Quarterly* see this as "both a governance failure and a strategic opportunity."[2]

And while most boards agree that succession planning is a fundamental responsibility, it is something that is frequently discussed but rarely implemented. A 2016 survey conducted by Nonprofit HR revealed that 59 percent of nonprofit organizations do *not* have a formal succession plan for senior leadership.[3] The good news is that the percentage has decreased significantly—from 69 percent in 2013—as many nonprofits realize the benefits of planning for change while there is ample time to think strategically about their institutions' futures and the kind of leadership that will be required.

With this mind-set regarding the change, an executive search can result in not only finding new staff leadership but also strengthening board leadership. And the benefits do not stop here; a strategically conceived and effectively managed executive search can produce many ancillary dividends: clarity about the museum's priorities, opportunities to identify new board leaders, an invigorated and empowered staff, and a broader base of community support. This book and the accompanying templates will help you make the most of this significant moment of change in the life of your institution, whether you have had the opportunity to plan for an executive search or not. And if you are among the growing number of boards that have been proactive in developing a succession plan, we applaud your foresight!

With or without pre-planning, an executive search is extremely time-consuming. Nevertheless, boards must resist the pressure to fill the vacant executive position quickly, because imposing a tight timeline increases the likelihood of skipping important steps, overlooking critical issues, and making an unsound choice. The executive director of a nonprofit support center advises, "Boards must realize the importance of their hiring decision and make sure they have enough time to do it right."[4] *Executive Transitions* will help the board focus its time and energy on meeting the immediate need of filling the leadership void, select the best new director, and orient him or her for success in the long term.

A variety of sources underscore the fact that executive transition is a regular occurrence in nonprofit governance. A 2004 study of 2,200 nonprofit leaders supported by the Annie E. Casey Foundation found that 65 percent planned to leave their positions within five years.[5] A 2006 CompassPoint survey of 1,900 nonprofit executives revealed that 75 percent intended to leave within the same period.[6] More recently, BoardSource reported that 50 percent of nonprofit boards will be engaged in an executive search in the next five years.[7] The average tenure for nonprofit executive directors is six years; for museum directors, that figure is somewhere between four and six years. A 2008 leadership seminar for museum directors offered by the American Association (now Alliance) of Museums (AAM) revealed that the annual turnover in accredited museums was 15 percent, as compared with 9 percent in the nonprofit sector.[8] On average, AAM's online JobHQ posts more than two hundred executive director positions per year.

So executive transition must be seen as a fact of life for museum boards. Viewing it in this way can reduce some of the pressure and stress felt by the Search Committee and the entire museum family. The executive search process is intense, but it need not be exhausting. The considerations are complex, but they need not be confusing. In fact, this process can provide the opportunity for board and staff members to imagine a new future for their museum.

NOTES

1. Curtis R. Welling and John H. Vogel, "A Practical (and Possibly Provocative) Approach to Leadership Transitions," *Nonprofit Quarterly*, May 21, 2015.

2. Ibid.

3. Nonprofit HR, "2016 Nonprofit Employment Practices Survey," accessed July 27, 2017, www.nonprofithr.com/wp-content/uploads/2016/04/2016NEPSurvey-final.pdf.

4. Jan Masaoka, executive director, Support Center for Nonprofit Management, interview by Sean Bailey, *Philanthropy Journal Online*, July 1997.

5. Managance Consulting, *The Nonprofit Executive Leadership and Transitions Survey 2004* (Baltimore, MD: Annie E. Casey Foundation, 2004), accessed July 27, 2017, http://www.aecf.org/m/resourcedoc/aecf-NonProfitExecutiveLeadershipSurvey-2004.pdf.

6. Jeanne Peters and Timothy Wolfred, *Daring to Lead: Nonprofit Executive Directors and Their Work Experience* (Oakland, CA: CompassPoint Nonprofit Services, 2001).

7. "Executive Transition," BoardSource, accessed July 27, 2017, https://boardsource.org/fundamental-topics-of-nonprofit-board-service/executive-transition/.

8. American Association (now Alliance) of Museums workshop, 2008.

1

Preparing for a New Future

PLAN THE SEARCH PROCESS

Template 1: Search Process Timeline

It has been said that those who fail to plan, plan to fail. Outlining the process before you begin is critical. **Template 1: Search Process Timeline** will help the board and the Search Committee allocate time and resources for a successful search and a smooth transition. This investment in planning will ensure that there is enough time to complete each step in the executive search.

The **Search Process Timeline** identifies thirty-two discrete tasks and where they fit into the overall schedule.

The template takes each of the steps, with suggested durations, and places them on a PERT (Program Evaluation and Resource Technique) chart (figure 1.1). The steps in the process will not always occur in the order in which they appear in the timeline. For example, if the board knows the director is leaving, it may develop an interim leadership plan before announcing the director's resignation or termination. Some steps may occur simultaneously, such as when the Search Committee writes the job description while the Personnel Committee is developing the compensation package. The **Search Process Timeline** is based on the idea of a critical path. To find the shortest path from the beginning of the process to the end, some tasks (called "critical tasks") must be completed. You cannot skip these tasks and move on to the next; if you delay a critical task, it will affect all the dates that follow it. Tasks that are not critical can be deleted or delayed without affecting the rest of the process. The timeline gives recommended durations (in seven-day weeks) for each step. You can change the start date and/or duration of any step, thereby altering the entire schedule (see the online Help Manual accessible through the app). **Template 1: Search Process Timeline** shows how the tasks fit into the groundwork, search, and transition stages.

An alternative to the critical path approach is to create more basic diagrammatic charts showing what happens at different points in the search process and using arrows to indicate how steps are related. You can start with the steps outlined in the template, identify those that are applicable to your search process, and lay them out in sequence.

Whichever approach you take, creating an interim leadership plan is essential—and the sooner, the better. There are many unknowns when a director leaves, so internal and external stakeholders need to have a general sense of how the process will unfold, who will assume responsibility for various tasks, how ongoing projects will move forward, and what the anticipated timeline will be. It's not unusual for a top candidate to choose another position, making the process take far longer than anticipated, so the plan should set a direction without setting a conclusion. Since the search process is a work in progress, the plan must be as well. As soon as the plan is outlined, begin meeting with those who will be most directly involved—first those on the interim leadership team, then the board, senior staff, full staff, volunteers, and community partners.

Template 1: Search Process Timeline

	Step #	Task	Begins on Day	Days Duration
Plan and Budget	1	Board chair announces departure of previous director.	1	1
	2	Board allocates human and financial resources for search process using **Template 1: Search Process Timeline** and **Template 2: Search Budget** and appoints administrator to perform the administrative tasks of the search.	7	7
	3	Board establishes parameters of interim leadership plan.	14	14
Form the Search Committee	4	Board selects Search Committee using **Template 3A: Search Committee Chair Job Description** and **Template 3B: Search Committee Job Description.**	28	14
	5	Board announces appointment of Search Committee, outlines interim leadership plan, and provides interim leader with materials identified in **appendix A.**	42	1
Conduct Institutional Audit	6	Search Committee meets to identify those whose perspectives are needed; administrator sends them **Template 4: Institutional Audit** and allows two weeks to complete.	43	14
	7	Administrator sends **Report 4: Institutional Audit Summary** to Search Committee members.	57	7
	8	Search Committee conducts retreat using **appendix C** and administrator summarizes outcomes using **Template 5: Search Committee Retreat Guide.**	64	1
Envision and Describe the Next Leader	9	Search Committee meets to envision new leader using **Template 6: Professional Skills and Personal Qualities** and writes job description.	65	7
	10	Personnel Committee develops compensation package, including salary range, benefits, and relocation assistance.	65	7
	11	Search Committee completes **Template 7: Position Announcement,** posts position, and sources through professional networks.	72	14
Assess the Candidates	12	Search Committee receives applications and establishes process for reviewing them using **Template 8: Candidate Assessment Initial Review.**	86	28
	13	Search Committee meets to select top candidates.	114	2
	14	Search Committee sends letters and information packets to top candidates and letters to remaining applicants thanking them for their interest in the position.	116	3
	15	Search Committee members make initial screening calls to top candidates and create a short list of candidates.	119	7
	16	Search Committee conducts interviews with short list by phone or videoconference using **Template 9: Interview Outline/Skills and Qualities Assessment** and identifies final candidates.	126	14
	17	Search Committee schedules and conducts in-person interviews for final candidates to visit the museum and meet board and staff members.	140	14
	18	Search Committee checks references of final candidates using **Template 10: Reference Check.**	154	7
	19	Search Committee meets to discuss references and select finalist(s).	161	1
Seal the Deal	20	Search Committee recommends finalist(s) to the board.	162	1
	21	Board meets to confirm/select top candidate.	163	1
	22	Representatives of Search Committee and Personnel Committee refine offer and write contract with advice of legal counsel.	164	7
	23	Search Committee chair presents offer to finalist.	171	7
	24	Search Committee negotiates terms when finalist accepts or extends offer to alternate candidate.	178	14
Orientation and Introductions	25	Search Committee and board make plans for orientation and transition using **Template 11: Transition Calendar.**	192	7
	26	Board announces appointment to staff and volunteers.	199	1
	27	Board and staff announce appointment to members, the community, and professional networks.	200	7
	28	Search Committee introduces director and family to the museum and the community.	207	14
	29	Board and staff provide director with museum information, policies, and procedures using **appendix A.**	221	7
Monitor Progress	30	Director, board chair, and Personnel Committee develop performance goals and objectives for the transition year.	228	28
	31	Director, board chair, and Personnel Committee measure progress and review performance goals and objectives, recalibrating as needed.	256	150
	32	Board chair and Personnel Committee conduct director's annual assessment.	406	

FIGURE 1.1
Search Process Timeline (Courtesy of the Museum Trustee Association)

PREPARE FOR THE TRANSITION

Skills the Board Needs

Good governance and communication skills are never more important than during a time of executive transition. It's essential to keep communication open and honest. This requires two things: 1) a structured process so board and staff members do not find themselves in situations where they need to respond on the fly; 2) an explicit statement about what does and does not need to remain confidential.

The board acquires skills with practice over time, so ongoing attention to governance routines will pay big dividends during the leadership transition. Assessment and oversight are especially critical responsibilities. Boards that regularly assess themselves and the director are better prepared to work through challenges, focusing on the most important issues. (For a mutual assessment of the board and the director, see *The Leadership Partnership*, volume 2 in the *Templates for Trustees* series.) Boards that understand their responsibility for oversight are better able to provide the leadership that is needed when there is a vacancy in the director's office.

Communication, Confidentiality, and Candor

Clear, open communication is essential because a change in executive leadership has implications for every member of the board, staff, and volunteer corps. It is bound to generate some anxiety within the ranks because it is human nature to fear the unknown. Secrets tend to increase the anxiety level, making it absolutely critical that the board communicates openly and regularly with the staff and volunteers—not only at the announcement of the previous director's departure and the new director's appointment but also throughout the search process. Everyone involved deserves access to accurate and timely information. Open lines of communication must run from the Search Committee to the board, from the board to the staff, and from the staff to the volunteers. If there is an interim director, he or she should serve as the liaison between the board and the staff.

Along with the need for communication comes the need for confidentiality. Those who serve on the Search Committee and interim leadership team will be privy to information that cannot be made public without jeopardizing the future of both the museum and potential candidates. For that reason, everyone involved in the search process should sign confidentiality statements when they agree to serve. Many who have engaged in executive searches maintain that confidentiality is the single most important aspect of the process. This simply cannot be emphasized enough to board and staff members. There must be a structured process for communication that explicitly states what must be kept confidential. And if a specific instance comes up that is not covered, the rule should be: When in doubt, do not violate any confidence!

Candor is also essential in sharing information with candidates and with search firms. Finances are one area where absolute honesty is paramount. If there are any concerns about sustainability, it is essential to shine a light on them rather than attempt to conceal them. Simply put, a new leader cannot be expected to solve problems he or she is not aware of. In interviews with final candidates, the Search Committee must be prepared to take a deep dive into the museum's budget, perhaps inviting the board treasurer or chair of the Finance Committee to contribute their perspectives.

Case in point: After conducting a national search, a regional history museum hired a well-qualified new director who moved across the country with her partner to assume the position. Within weeks of her arrival, it became clear that the financial picture was so bleak that it was going to be difficult to make payroll. This discovery led to other problems that were insurmountable, and within a few months the new director was gone and the museum's financial crisis was in the national spotlight.

Choosing a Facilitator

It takes an objective perspective and experience managing group dynamics to help museum insiders identify priorities and move toward consensus. Some boards are fortunate enough to have members who can lend this perspective and experience in the search process. The Executive Committee or the Governance Committee may be able to look around the board table and identify people who are skilled facilitators. These board members can be enlisted to help the Search Committee as needed throughout the process.

If no internal facilitators can be identified, the Search Committee should seek an outside facilitator. Those with a broader perspective can make the best use of available time and resources, keeping conversations oriented toward the future. If resources are limited and you can enlist the services of a consultant for just one part of the search process, we recommend the Institutional Assessment (in the groundwork stage). Bringing the Search Committee to a consensus on priorities that will lead to creating the job description and position announcement is the foundation on which the rest of the search process is built. Outside facilitation may also be particularly helpful if there is dissension among board and staff members or if the previous director left under negative circumstances. If you choose to hire a facilitator, be sure to include this expense in **Template 2: Search Budget**. Museums that can't afford this expense may be able to find an outside facilitator from a nonprofit support group. Colleagues on other boards can also lend a valuable perspective. It is not necessary for the facilitator to have museum experience, but experience in nonprofits is helpful.

The Departing Director's Role

The terms on which the previous director leaves have a profound impact on the character of the search process. On the most basic level, there are two scenarios: the director who decides to leave, and the director who is asked to leave. In reality, every situation is different, and there are many variations. A long-tenured director with a strong history may play a role in the transition or even in finding his or her successor. In either case, it is important to specify the ways in which he or she will contribute to the process and to acknowledge contributions, express thanks publicly and privately, invite him or her to make a list of major issues to be kept in mind, and then delicately but firmly suggest that the Search Committee will take the lead moving forward. A director with a shorter tenure who is moving to a new position will probably be focusing his or her energies there. Even if the departure is imminent, the exiting director probably has valuable perspectives on the leadership transition that can be gathered in an exit interview (see page 10).

Not only the Search Committee but candidates may wish to learn about the position from the standpoint of the previous director. If the director leaves under favorable circumstances and is willing to speak to candidates, the Search Committee can put them in touch with one another. Once a candidate has been selected as the new director, he or she will almost certainly want to talk to their predecessor. When the Search Committee informs the previous director of the hire, they can share contact information so the two leaders can be in touch.

A director who has been fired may leave a multitude of unresolved issues, making it difficult but essential to start the search process with a clean slate. With an abrupt change in leadership, the director most likely will not be involved at all. Even in this case, a small group of board members should thank the exiting director and explain that an interim leadership team will be taking responsibility for leading the museum from this point forward.

Whatever the circumstances or level of involvement, it is the responsibility of trustees to hear out the departing director in order to learn everything they need to know to move forward. This is crucial, because, at the end of the day, the search process is always board-driven, and the selection of a new director is ultimately a board decision.

CONSIDER HIRING A SEARCH FIRM

Boards have numerous opportunities to practice routine governance functions, such as budgeting and planning, but many boards, especially those with term limits, have little prior experience in exercising their responsibility to hire the director. Those boards may benefit from hiring an executive search firm, which can coach and support the Search Committee through the process and help it stay focused on the issues that are central to the hiring decision. Search firms maintain extensive databases of prospective candidates and can match individuals with specific positions. They can recruit people who are happily employed and not actively looking for a job, while it is not always comfortable for a Search Committee to do so. If the museum hires a candidate who does not work out in the first year, many search firms will repeat the search process without additional charge.

Executive search firms have two basic ways of structuring their fees: a consulting fee for services or a percentage (typically 35–40 percent) of the director's salary if, and only if, someone is hired for the position. Some search committees may choose the latter option to avoid paying fees for an unsuccessful search; however, many committees believe that a fee attached to a candidate's salary creates a potential conflict of interest and find that knowing the fee up front helps with budgeting. There is a wide range of fees depending on the size of the search firm and the scope of services. Boutique firms and individual search consultants may charge $40,000–$60,000, while large firms' fees may be in the neighborhood of $100,000.

The full scope of services typically includes an initial phone interview with the Search Committee; an onsite meeting to interview Search Committee members, staff members, and other stakeholders such as major donors;

leading the Search Committee through the process of writing a position announcement; sharing it with a network of colleagues across the country and posting it online and in print; reviewing applications, screening applicants, and conducting reference checks; presenting the Search Committee with a slate of prospective candidates and helping narrow it down to a short list; planning the interview process from the first round through the finalists; and helping to negotiate a salary and details of the employment agreement. In some cases, search firms also stay in touch with the board and the new director during the transition period. Some search firms will work on specific steps of the search process, such as sourcing the position announcement or doing reference checks, but many recommend a more comprehensive approach.

While a search firm may coach both the Search Committee and the candidates during the process, it is important to understand that the firm works for the institution, not the candidate. The committee must be absolutely satisfied that it has been presented with the best candidate for the job. It should never settle for a candidate just because the right one hasn't come along yet.

Once a search firm has been selected, the board enters into an agreement that establishes clear goals and expectations, clarifies the services to be provided, and outlines the roles and responsibilities of both the consultant and the Search Committee, as well as fees and payment schedule. One of the committee's first responsibilities is to describe the museum's current situation in detail so the consultant can fully understand the duties and qualifications of the position.

Asked what single point she tries to communicate to all of her clients, a search consultant says, "Honesty is absolutely essential." Although most people don't like to divulge the negatives, she stresses that search committees must trust her enough to share the bad news as well as the good. "You really need to treat me like a member of this family for the duration of this assignment," she says. If there was any dirty laundry, search firms need to know what the issues were and how they were resolved so they can accurately respond to any rumors candidates may have heard through the grapevine.

When and if a search firm is hired, the Search Committee must still be accessible throughout the process. The chair and committee members should be prepared to answer a variety of questions about details that might not seem important but are, in fact, crucial to matching candidates with the institution. Search Committee members must also make it a priority to be available when interviews are scheduled. It is an embarrassment and a waste of time to bring in a candidate when the necessary group is not present to conduct the interview. Understanding and agreeing to these requirements will help the Search Committee maximize the return on its investment from a search firm and help the consultants do their best work.

Some boards may not have the option of hiring a search firm because they cannot afford the additional expense. Others may be concerned that this approach would mean less involvement for the board. It is important to realize that hiring a search firm does not change the fact that the ultimate responsibility for the hiring decision rests squarely with the Search Committee and the board. Consultants will recommend a group of candidates, sharing the pros and cons of each, but they will not make the final decision.

2

The Groundwork Stage

During this phase of the executive transition, the board and Search Committee will use four templates:

- **Template 2: Search Budget** to allocate human and financial resources
- **Template 3A: Search Committee Chair Job Description** to identify a chair who will lead the process, and **Template 3B: Search Committee Job Description** to recruit committee members
- **Template 4: Institutional Audit** and **Report 4: Institutional Audit Summary** to identify the museum's strengths and weaknesses
- **Template 5: Search Committee Retreat Guide** to summarize the opportunities and challenges for the new director and current strategic priorities for the museum

THE DIRECTOR'S DEPARTURE

The executive transition officially begins when the director's departure is announced. If the director resigns, it is his or her responsibility to notify the board chair. The chair then notifies all board members immediately, in keeping with their fiduciary responsibility for the museum. In accepting the director's resignation, the board should ask for a reasonable period of notice—at least one month, and several months in the case of a planned retirement. As soon as the terms are agreed upon, the board chair should communicate with staff and volunteers. Donors, collaborators, and key community partners should also be notified promptly, each in the appropriate way (for example, personal phone calls to the museum's strongest supporters and emails to spokespeople for various groups). This is the board's only opportunity to shape the message it wants to send before word leaks out.

A public statement from the board chair can simply say that the director will be leaving and include the date of his or her departure and good wishes for future endeavors or retirement, as the case may be. It is not necessary to go into detail about the reasons for the departure, whether positive or negative. If the director is leaving for a new position, it is the responsibility and prerogative of the new employer to announce the appointment. If the director is leaving on unpleasant terms, it is critically important to the future of the institution and all the individuals involved that both the director and the board decide to part well. Confidentiality agreements signed by the departing director as well as the board chair can clarify what will and will not be shared.

Once the initial news has been shared, create a more comprehensive messaging plan with the help of board members who have experience in communications and public relations. Consider key messages and talking points such as who will be acting as the interim leader, the process and timeline for the executive search, who to contact for more information about ongoing projects, and how search updates will be shared throughout the transition. Internal stakeholders (board, staff, volunteers, and members) and external parties (donors, community partners, local media, and state/regional/national museum organizations) will have different questions, so tailor communications to each group.

Whatever the terms of the departure, the board should ask the director to provide:

- The current administrative calendar, including performance reviews
- Dates of regularly scheduled meetings with staff and community groups
- Expiration and renewal dates of all leases and contracts
- Pay periods and other recurring dates
- A contact list of key stakeholders, including funders, advisors (legal, accounting, and real estate), professional organizations, community organizations, and colleagues at other museums
- A description of the organization of his or her office, filing system, computer programs and files, keys, and locks

If possible, the departing director should complete all personnel performance reviews that are due within the quarter. Staff members will receive a fairer evaluation, and the new director will appreciate having current reviews available when he or she comes on board.

Exit Interview

Often the departing director can add a valuable perspective by helping the Search Committee understand the position. An exit interview should be conducted by a member of the Search Committee who is in a position to elicit honest, constructive answers—someone who has a rapport with and respect for the departing executive. If this conversation takes place before the Search Committee retreat, the director's feedback can be factored in with that of the board and staff members.

The exit interview can run parallel to the Institutional Audit, asking the director to reflect on the museum's human, financial, and physical resources and the community's support. Or it can be an open-ended conversation that revolves around the following questions:

- In your experience, what have been the greatest strengths and weaknesses of the staff?
- How could the director-staff relationship be strengthened?
- In your experience, what have been the greatest strengths and weaknesses of the board?
- How could the executive-board relationship be strengthened?
- Given your knowledge of the communities the museum serves, what do you see as the greatest needs and opportunities?
- Looking into the future, do you see any red flags in the areas of finances, personnel, facilities, or external conditions?
- What was your greatest accomplishment? What was your biggest disappointment?
- What were the most satisfying and the most frustrating aspects of the job?
- If it were up to you, what kind of leader would you hire to replace yourself?
- If you were asked to advise the incoming director, what two things would you emphasize?
- How would you characterize the museum's reputation in the field?

DEVELOP THE SEARCH BUDGET

Template 2: Search Budget

Before beginning the search process, the board should allocate financial resources using **Template 2: Search Budget**. This spreadsheet identifies needed resources, where they will come from, and how they will be allocated.

TEMPLATE 2: SEARCH BUDGET

	Cost	# of Months	Monthly Budget	Actual	Variance
Sources of Funds					
Contributions					
Savings in salaries and benefits					0
Prior director salary				0	0
Prior director expenses				0	0
Prior director benefits				0	0
Other				0	0
General budget/operating funds	0				
Total Sources of Funds			0	0	0
Uses of Funds					
Consultant fees					0
Executive search firm					0
Meeting facilitator					0
Executive coach					0
Staff increases					0
Interim director compensation					
Additional compensation to current staff				0	0
				0	0
Severance compensation					0
Search Committee expenses					0
Advertising fees					0
Video conference service					0
Postage					0
Hospitality					0
Travel expenses					0
Other					0
Other				0	0
Total Uses of Funds			0	0	0

Sources of funds may include new revenues, such as contributions earmarked for the search, as well as previously budgeted amounts that can be redirected. Identify funds that had been budgeted elsewhere, such as compensation or reimbursable expenses for the prior executive director or unexpended or carry-over funds from the prior year.

Uses of funds—the search expenses—will include the purchase of this publication, search consultants' fees, advertising, postage, and printing costs. Other costs might include farewell events for a director who leaves on good terms or a severance package for one who is asked to resign; food and beverages for meetings, interviews, and receptions; coaching services for the new leader; and increased accounting or legal costs. Travel and hospitality costs for candidates are often underestimated. It's not unusual for final candidates to make a second trip with their spouse or partner, so include generous figures in your budget. Remember that arrangements are often made with short notice; do not assume bargain fares in the budget.

Update the **Search Budget** monthly, comparing estimated and actual expenses. The Search Committee should provide the board with a revised budget at each regular board meeting.

WEIGH INTERIM LEADERSHIP OPTIONS

If the outgoing leader is leaving on good terms and can stay on until the new director is appointed, this can be a great benefit to the successor as well as the staff. If this arrangement is not possible, appointing an interim leader will give the board and the Search Committee time to focus on the important task of choosing a new executive director without the pressure of feeling like the clock is ticking. Some boards may plan to fill the vacancy quickly, avoiding the need to appoint a temporary executive, but things rarely go according to plan. A study of interim executive leadership patterns in museums reports it takes an average of six to nine months from the departure of one director to the hiring of another, and it might well be a year from the date the departing director gives notice until the new director actually begins work.[1]

In general, a well-chosen interim leader is better able to maintain momentum than a team of either board or staff members, all of whom will have to take on additional responsibilities during the transition period. The board should consider the following options for interim leadership:

- *Hire an interim director from outside the institution.* Nonprofit CEOs who have retired or are between positions are often happy to take on temporary assignments. Experienced executives from other fields—especially non-profits—can provide effective leadership during a transition. In fact, some individual consultants specialize in interim leadership. A study of interim leadership patterns found that although smaller museums thought this option was too expensive, museums that did employ an outsider found that the strategy was cost-effective, provided for a smooth transition, lent objectivity to the process, and helped resolve difficult issues.[2]
- *Hire a consulting firm.* Nonprofit executive management consulting firms often maintain a cadre of people who provide interim leadership services. Management consultants in your community are a cost-effective alternative to national firms because they avoid the cost of temporary relocation. They also have the benefit of knowing the local culture and have experience networking in your city and region.
- *Find pro bono leadership help.* You may find that a board member or community member with experience in nonprofit management is willing to volunteer his or her services on a short-term basis. An art museum that was conducting a search had a board member with arts management experience. Even though she lived fifty miles away in an adjacent state, she volunteered to spend two days a week leading the staff during the search process. If you take this route, remember that clearly articulated expectations are just as important in an agreement with a volunteer as with a paid consultant.

- *Appoint a staff member.* Those who know the museum well can make excellent interim directors. Deputy directors and department heads are good choices, especially if they do not want to be a candidate for the director's position. One of the first conversations with a staff member who is being considered for the interim role should be about whether that person is interested in being considered as a candidate. If so, this could compromise both their ability to lead and their candidacy. If a staff member who serves as the interim director is—or becomes—a candidate, this must be handled explicitly and with sensitivity. If this person is not chosen as the director, it may be difficult to continue in another position at the institution. (For a discussion of the pros and cons of internal candidates, see pages 38–39.) When a staff member assumes responsibility for interim leadership, it's important to remember that someone else must temporarily assume his or her normal responsibilities.
- *Appoint a board member.* The chair, past chair, or other board leaders may be willing and able to step up to the plate at this critical time. However, we recommend this solution as a last resort, especially in the case of the board president who has critical responsibilities that complement the director's own. In addition to familiarity with the museum, management and leadership skills are essential. If a board member is selected as interim director, he or she must be fully prepared to step aside when the new director is hired.

Each interim leadership option has pros and cons. An internal staff member knows the museum and the personalities well and can keep up the momentum if systems are in place and things are moving smoothly. An outside leader can bring a fresh perspective and make decisions without the baggage of knowing what led to the previous director's departure. A member of the board can bring the big-picture perspective of governance, although he or she will need to put on a very different hat to work in a staff capacity.

In addition to management skills, an interim leader should be a good listener who can serve as a sounding board for the staff and a collaborator with the board. Flexibility is also key because search processes often extend beyond their estimated timelines, and one never knows what unanticipated events might occur. One interim director of a small local history museum was awakened by a call at 2:00 a.m. to learn that a one-hundred-year flood had left the entire collections storage area under two feet of water! This drastically altered her day-to-day priorities as well as the schedule of the Search Committee, whose members joined the bucket brigade.

Whoever serves as the interim leader, they must step out of the leadership role as easily as they step into it. Relinquishing the position graciously and effectively is one of the most important and challenging tasks of an interim leader. A consultant who provides interim leadership services says that while she is leading staff and board members, she is preparing them for the arrival of another leader. She may stay on to facilitate the transition, but she quickly steps into the background, letting the new director make the decisions. If staff members come to her with questions, she refers them to their new leader. When outside constituents call, she says, "I'd like to introduce you to the new director. Can I connect you with him?"

Boards often wonder what an interim leader will cost, and, of course, this depends on roles and responsibilities. Every museum has different needs. In some cases, the interim director's primary role may be to act as a change agent, addressing issues that will build a firm foundation for the new director; in others, they will keep things moving along on an even keel with the staff and volunteers while the Search Committee does its work. Some interim directors may participate actively in the process, helping the Search Committee to develop the job description, post the position announcement, screen applicants, and orient the new director. Depending on the circumstances, these responsibilities may involve full- or part-time work. As a guideline, the search budget should include an amount for interim leadership that is in line with the minimum salary that will be offered to the new director.

Supporting Interim Leadership

What can the board do to facilitate the work of an interim leader? First, negotiate an employment agreement that is clear to both parties. Not all of the former director's responsibilities will necessarily be passed on to the interim leader. The contract or letter of agreement must outline a commitment that is clear but not finite and has enough flexibility to allow the search to unfold in its own time. One search that was expected to take three months wound up taking twenty-three! So specify a minimum duration based on the Search Committee's best-case scenario and a maximum duration that allows for unanticipated delays, such as a top candidate who accepts another position. Include a provision that either party can terminate the agreement with a certain period of notice.

As soon as the terms have been agreed upon, provide the interim leader with all of the information he or she will need to do the job effectively and efficiently. Alternatively, encourage the interim leader to create a list and work with staff members to assemble necessary materials. This can provide a good opportunity for the interim and staff members to get to know one another. Consider creating an executive transition USB flash drive or a secure folder on the museum's server with copies of the documents listed in appendix A.

Boards can support interim directors and make the most of their contributions by creating a reporting structure in which the interim leader works with a small core of board leadership. For example, two or three members of the Executive Committee and/or chairs of other key committees can help fill in gaps in institutional history, identify current issues, and anticipate potential problems. They can also facilitate decision-making and help keep things moving along smoothly and efficiently.

Staff members can also facilitate interim leadership if department chairs submit updated lists of their current major responsibilities over the upcoming six to twelve months and provide regular progress reports. This procedure will help the interim leader to coordinate work details during the transition; it will also help the new director to understand staff responsibilities when he or she arrives.

Professionals outside the museum can provide the board and interim leader with specific expertise. Consider the following options:

- If you have a relationship with an accounting firm, talk with your accountant about his or her assessment of the museum's current financial position and any extraordinary upcoming needs. If your museum does not have an external accountant or auditor, hire a certified public accountant (CPA) to review the museum's finances and brief the interim leader on financial operations.
- If you have an attorney who specializes in personnel issues on your board, ask for advice in drafting a contract or letter of agreement with the interim leader. If your board doesn't include an attorney or human resources professional, hire one to assist the Search Committee.

Once the terms of the agreement have been clarified, announce the appointment of the interim leader to the staff and volunteers and field questions to ensure that everyone is operating under the same expectations. Make it clear that the interim director is the primary contact person for staff and volunteers and that he or she will have full authority for decision-making and independent action until a new director is on board. Other staff members may be temporarily reassigned to support the interim director or maintain the momentum of in-progress projects the previous director had been working on. In either case, it will be helpful to both board and staff members to have a roster of all those with interim assignments, including contact info and specific areas of responsibility during the transition period.

In the absence of an interim director, a board leader must make him or herself accessible during the transition period. One museum was without anyone in the director's office for two months. During that time, the board chair made a point of stopping by the museum each week to check in with senior staff members. Regular board presence is especially important to staff and volunteers during times of executive transition, inspiring confidence and dispelling rumors.

FORM THE SEARCH COMMITTEE

The board chair, Executive Committee, and other board members, as needed, will initiate the search process by recruiting and nominating members of the Search Committee, an ad hoc committee charged with recruiting, selecting, and orienting the museum's next leader. The committee should be small enough to function efficiently and large enough to incorporate all the necessary perspectives—at least half a dozen members, and certainly no more than ten. Too large a committee can hamper efficient scheduling and meaningful dialogue, both within the committee and with the candidates. An odd number of members can prove helpful in cases where opinions are divided. The committee should also be chosen with the museum's strategic priorities in mind because the composition of the committee speaks volumes to prospective candidates. They will certainly notice the distribution of gender, race, and socioeconomic backgrounds of Search Committee members.

Generally, the nominations process starts at an Executive Committee meeting or a full board meeting. Whatever the case, it is important to identify *what* you're looking for before identifying *who* you're looking for. Above all, this is a situation that benefits from broad-minded individuals, not those who already have the answers.

Template 3A: Search Committee Chair Job Description

The single most important decision the board will make is selecting the chair of the Search Committee. This individual will lay the foundation and set the tone for the entire transition process. All too often, boards make this decision too quickly and casually. It is best to start with a list of the traits you want in the chair, and then identify individuals who possess the experience, skills, and leadership styles outlined in **Template 3A: Search Committee Chair Job Description**. This template, which articulates the purpose, responsibilities, and attributes of the position, can be modified to reflect special considerations or needs that are unique to the museum and the communities it serves.

A critical question is: Who has the time to give at this important juncture and the flexibility to accommodate a variety of eventualities? It's essential to allow for different scenarios because, in spite of careful planning and best efforts, it's impossible to know how the search process will unfold. The ability to prioritize is also essential. One Search Committee chair was determined to a find the "perfect" candidate, someone who could do it all, and therefore she did not lead the committee in prioritizing the needed skills. When it came time to interview candidates, it was too late to talk about priorities, so subjective qualities like personalities muddied the evaluation process.

In addition to being able to establish priorities, the Search Committee chair must be someone who inspires confidence in others, whose work will be trusted, whose decisions will be respected, and who has no personal agenda. Because communication is so critical during times of transition, it is important that this person be able to strike a balance between confidentiality and secrecy. Trust is the key to maintaining internal and external relationships during the search process. Ideally, the chair will be someone who has demonstrated leadership skills in the past. One of the dividends of the search process is that it presents a wonderful opportunity to "audition" new board leadership. Since the board chair and the new director will work together so closely, the board chair should not serve as chair of the Search Committee. That said, it is not unusual for the Search Committee chair to become the next board chair, especially if she or he establishes a good rapport with the new director during the search process.

TEMPLATE 3A: SEARCH COMMITTEE CHAIR JOB DESCRIPTION

{[Museum Name]}

{[Mission Statement]}

Purpose

- Recruit and recommend to the board the top candidate(s) for the museum's new {[Title]} and plan transition to ensure the {[Title]}'s success
- This ad hoc committee will be in place until a new {[Title]} is hired and on board, a period estimated at six to nine months.

Responsibilities

- Identify internal and external perspectives needed on the Search Committee
- Identify individuals with those perspectives and assess their ability to serve
- Clarify expectations and recruit six to eight members who collectively have the necessary perspectives, vision, skills, experience, and personality styles
- Create agendas and lead all Search Committee meetings
- Communicate regularly with board chair, who will be the liaison with board committees and the full board
- Act as the official spokesperson for the Search Committee, providing updates on the search process and progress to museum staff members, external stakeholders, and community members
- Guide assessment of candidates and bring Search Committee members to consensus on the top candidate(s) for the new {[Title]}
- Work with Personnel Committee and legal advisor to create compensation package
- Extend offer to final candidate on behalf of the museum
- Plan ways to support the new director in his or her first year on the job
- Other

Attributes

- Demonstrated leadership skills
- Understanding of the importance of confidentiality as well as the pitfalls of secrecy
- Ability to inspire confidence in others
- A broad-minded approach that is open to a variety of solutions
- Patience and a tendency to avoid coming to premature conclusions
- Time to devote and flexibility to accommodate a variety of eventual timelines
- Strategic thinker
- Ability to prioritize among competing goods
- Capacity to build consensus
- Well respected by fellow board members
- Other

Template 3B: Search Committee Job Description

One of the first jobs for the Search Committee chair is to work with board leaders to:

- identify the internal and external perspectives needed on the committee
- identify individuals who represent those perspectives
- assess their ability to serve on the committee based on experience, leadership skills, and time availability

They can start by asking the following questions:

- What skills are needed—for example, strategic thinking, decision-making, consensus building, and human re-sources? Consider personnel managers, attorneys, and strategic planners who are on your board or are friends of the museum.
- What leadership perspectives are needed? Consider members of board committees, such as Executive, Finance, Human Resources, and Governance and Board Development, as well as ad hoc committees and task forces.
- What institutional life cycle perspectives can shape the history and vision for the museum? For history, include former board and task force members, retired staff, former directors, founders, and long-time volunteers. For vision, include new board leaders who can introduce fresh viewpoints and suggest expanded options for the museum's future.
- What stakeholder perspectives are needed? In addition to board members, consider museum members, volunteers, and target audiences—both served and underserved communities.
- What strategic alliances must be considered? Consider staff or board at other museums, project partners, and arts and humanities councils.

As a list of names starts to emerge, keep in mind two related considerations: the perspectives, expertise, skills, and personality styles that each *individual* member would bring and the *collective* profile of the entire committee. Ideally, diverse perspectives will contribute to a collective vision of the museum's future. A balance of personality styles and skills is also necessary on a committee charged with identifying the museum's new leader. The Search Committee chair will be in a position to draw out comments and approaches from all members of the committee—listeners as well as speakers, traditionalists and innovators, consensus builders and devil's advocates.

One place to look for Search Committee members is around the board table. A board roster may provide answers to the first three questions listed above. Consider special circumstances, based on major projects on the horizon. For example, if the museum is involved in a capital campaign, it may be important to include the Capital Campaign Committee chair. If it is in the middle of a building project, the perspectives of a member of the Building Committee would be helpful. If you decide the process would benefit from outside perspectives, the latter two questions identify a second tier of individuals and institutions to tap. For example, if the museum is affiliated with a magnet school, the school principal or president of the Parent-Teacher-Student Association may be a good addition to the Search Committee.

Expectations have a profound effect on our experiences, and time is one of the biggest commitments required of the Search Committee. If you tell prospective members, "This won't take much of your time," you're not likely to get much of their time. If you tell them, "We're looking for people who can participate actively in a process that's critical to the future of the museum," you will likely receive their active and enthusiastic participation. **Template 3B: Search Committee Job Description** outlines the committee's purpose, membership, projected timeline, responsibilities, and expectations so prospective members will understand the roles and terms to which they are agreeing.

TEMPLATE 3B: SEARCH COMMITTEE JOB DESCRIPTION

{[Museum Name]}

{[Mission Statement]}

Purpose

- Recruit and recommend to the board the top candidate(s) for the museum's new director and plan transition to ensure this person's success
- This ad hoc committee will be in place until a new director is hired and on board, a period estimated at six to nine months

Membership

- Six to eight members, which may include board, staff, and museum members, as well as volunteers and community partners

Responsibilities

- Identify internal and external perspectives needed to clarify the museum's current situation
- Envision professional skills and personal qualities needed in the next leader in light of the current situation
- Articulate qualifications and opportunities of the position, advertise, and source among professional networks
- Screen potential candidates
- Participate in candidate interviews by phone, video conference, and on site, writing a brief personal assessment of each candidate
- Debrief on all candidates, articulating recommendations and reasons for them
- Check references and come to consensus regarding top candidate(s)
- Plan ways to support the new director in his or her first year on the job
- Other

Expectations

- Maintain complete confidentiality throughout the search and transition process
- Protect the privacy of all applicants and prospective candidates
- Guard the reputation of the museum by holding all Search Committee discussions in confidence
- Participate in all Search Committee meetings—by phone and face-to-face
- Speak openly and honestly, even if it means disagreeing with others
- Learn about the {[Museum Name]}'s collections, operations, bylaws, policies, and programs as they relate to the director's role
- Other

Questions they may have included:

- What is the anticipated timeframe for the search process?
- What responsibility does the Search Committee have?
- When and how will the committee meet?
- Who will be leading the process?
- What am I expected to contribute?

Staff on the Search Committee

Opinions on how to best incorporate staff perspectives in the executive search process are strong and divided. Some seasoned governance experts assert that strong boards will welcome the active participation of staff members on the Search Committee, believing that their perspectives are an essential part of the leadership equation. Others are of the opinion that staff members should not be involved in the search process except to be updated at key junctures. In the end, each board will have to make this important decision after considering the following questions:

- How large is the museum? Are staff members generally inside the loop, or does a large bureaucracy separate them from board and executive leadership?
- Is staff empowerment a significant part of the museum's culture?
- Is there a cadre of experienced and respected senior staff members whose perspectives are needed and helpful in the search for a new leader?
- Given the climate surrounding the previous director's departure, how critical is it to build a bridge to the staff at this time?

The board should consider the pros and cons of staff involvement thoughtfully. Staff members certainly have a crucial voice that can help the Search Committee to understand the needs of the institution. Their perspective is based on day-to-day involvement with the director and a working knowledge of the museum. Their cooperation is critical during times of executive transition, and involving one or two staff members can help the rest of their colleagues to feel enfranchised. Staff members are also instrumental when it comes time to plan visits with final candidates.

However, some boards may be concerned that putting staff members in the position of selecting their future supervisor can undermine the reporting structure and cause problems down the road. It should be made clear to everyone involved—from the Search Committee to the staff—that while staff members may be in the position of recommending the new director, they do not bear the responsibility for that decision; the board does.

Staff members who are appointed to the Search Committee generally serve in an advisory capacity, sometimes as nonvoting members. They may be invited to participate in some, but not all, of the committee meetings. Whatever the case, they are bound by the same rules of confidentiality as other Search Committee members. Since staff members who are close to the search process will be privy to information about their new boss, everyone must know—and be reminded—that those on the Search Committee have pledged their confidentiality.

However they participate in the search process, staff members should always have opportunities to meet final candidates who come for interviews. These introductions are mutually beneficial. Staff can learn what different candidates have to offer, and candidates can learn the perspectives of staff and volunteers. Some museums schedule group interviews with staff members. Others ask individual staff members to give candidates tours of exhibitions and behind-the-scenes areas. One museum invited department heads to interview all candidates who came for interviews. The Search Committee chair then talked with each staff member individually and brought his or her feedback to the committee. As the circle of staff members widens, it's important to remind everyone that confidentiality is required at this stage of the process as well. Whenever staff members meet final candidates, they should sign confidentiality statements.

The bottom line is that while the selection of a new director is a board decision, at some point staff participation will help the Search Committee to make its best decision. Another way of gathering staff input is to ask senior staff to complete **Template 4: Institutional Audit**. Smaller museums may decide to give the assessment to all staff members. However it is accomplished, there needs to be a significant moment when staff members from different departments within the museum have the opportunity to talk with the Search Committee about their views of what is most needed in their new leader. Including staff and volunteers in the process will help build the relationship with the new executive on a secure foundation.

Involving Those Outside the Museum

Individuals outside the board and museum may also have valuable perspectives about the kind of leader the museum needs in light of its place in the larger community. In some cases, they may even be in a position to recommend prospective candidates.

Non–board members on a Search Committee need to be oriented to the institution with information about its mission, vision, strategic plan, and financial health. In order to participate fully in the search, they need background information that will help them understand the museum's current situation and future goals. A new board member orientation packet is a good source of this information along with recent collateral material, such as print and online media describing current programs and services.

We do not recommend including donors on the Search Committee because their perspective can have an undue influence on the process and the outcome. The committee can factor in donor views by asking members to have conversations with funders or by asking one or two key funders to complete **Template 4: Institutional Audit**. Their responses will be tabulated with "other" responses.

Search Committee Standards

Everyone who serves on the Search Committee must agree to be bound by a common set of ethics; otherwise, the process and the outcome can turn out to be personal and public disasters. Complete confidentiality is absolutely essential. Each committee member—board, staff, or community representative—is bound by the highest level of trust. Each candidate who applies for the position is in a position of great vulnerability. That is why the identity of all candidates, discussions about them, interviews, and the reasoning of the Search Committee must be and forever remain completely confidential. Remember, the candidate you want may be gainfully and happily employed elsewhere, and his or her ability to maintain that relationship is affected by the way the candidacy is handled.

It bears mentioning that confidentiality is very different from secrecy. Secrecy during times of change breeds unrest and distrust. The Search Committee has a responsibility to museum stakeholders as well as to candidates. It must speak with a common voice, communicating with staff and other internal and external audiences throughout the search process and keeping them informed of progress. Instead of guarding information or dispensing it on a "need-to-know" basis, the committee should share any information about the search process that could boost morale and build a climate of support for the new leader.

In addition to confidentiality, other issues must be considered and addressed. Chief among them is who will be the official spokesperson for the museum during the transition period. Generally, the Search Committee chair would keep stakeholders informed and answer any questions about the search process; the board chair would speak to other ongoing museum issues.

In rare cases, a member of the Search Committee may be permitted to become a candidate if the process does not yield a suitable candidate. This requires very clear guidelines to prevent conflict of interest. The Search Committee member must resign immediately from the committee and go through all of the same vetting and interview processes as other candidates. See "Consider Internal Candidates" on pages 38–39 for other issues and guidelines.

Interim Leadership Teams

In addition to the Search Committee, the board may form an interim leadership team that can advise the interim director on strategic decisions, such as whether key hires should be made before the arrival of a new director. This can avoid putting undue burdens on current staff and help the new director to hit the ground running rather than spending time filling vacant positions.[3] A few trustees can also support the interim director to fill in any gaps in history, identify current issues and potential problems, and maintain momentum.

Along with a board interim leadership team, a small group of senior staff members may serve on an operational team charged with keeping things moving smoothly. If there are multiple teams, it is essential to clarify the function, composition, and authority of each. The Search Committee is focused on identifying, recruiting, and cultivating candidates while the board and staff interim leadership teams are concerned with keeping operations running smoothly. If one team serves both functions, as may be the case in small museums, it's essential for members to be clear about what mode they are in.

TAKE STOCK

The board is but one group of stakeholders that will be involved in identifying what kind of leadership the museum needs at this stage of its institutional life. The Institutional Audit begins by gathering quantitative feedback from key stakeholders. **Template 4: Institutional Audit** and **Template 5: Search Committee Retreat Guide** will gather and analyze information about the museum in four key areas: human resources, financial resources, physical resources, and community support.

Template 4: Institutional Audit

This assessment is designed specifically to help the Search Committee prioritize needs; it is not a strategic planning process. If your museum has engaged in a planning process within the last year, the Search Committee may be able to simply talk through the issues covered in the Institutional Audit. If your museum does not have a recent strategic plan, this will be a critical step for both the Search Committee and prospective candidates. (For an in-depth discussion of the pros and cons of creating a strategic plan before hiring a new director, see *Strategic Thinking and Planning*, the fourth volume in the Museum Trustee Association's *Templates for Trustees* series.)

To explore the museum's current situation from many angles, the Search Committee, full board, senior staff members, and perhaps outside stakeholders such as funders and community partners will be asked to complete a survey. Their feedback will be compiled, summarized, and discussed at a Search Committee retreat. It will provide an important foundation for the entire search process, helping the committee to start with a clean slate and determine the current priorities for the museum and its new leader.

Template 4: Institutional Audit asks this diverse group of stakeholders to agree or disagree with twenty-four statements in four broad categories.

The Search Committee will identify those whose perspectives will be valuable in determining the museum's current strengths and weaknesses, as well as opportunities and challenges on the horizon. The administrator will share the link to the survey with respondents who are members of the board or Search Committee, as well as staff and community members who are identified as having a valuable perspective on the museum. Once the administrator

Template 4: Institutional Audit

I. Human Resources
    1. The size and experience of the staff are adequate to fulfill the museum's mission.
    2. The staff has a positive attitude and works well as a team.
    3. The board has a clear understanding of its role in governing the museum and the necessary experience and leadership to do so.
    4. The board and the staff have an effective working relationship.
    5. The museum has a knowledgeable and dependable volunteer corps.
    6. The board, staff, and volunteer corps reflect the communities the museum aims to serve.
II. Financial Resources
    1. Earned income generates appropriate support for the museum's facilities, operations, exhibitions, and programs.
    2. Museum membership provides a sustainable source of revenue and support.
    3. Board and development staff members work in concert to cultivate and grow the donor base.
    4. The museum is able to generate support for temporary exhibits and other special projects through grants and private and corporate funding.
    5. The museum has an investment policy that generates appropriate returns to provide for the museum's current and future financial health.
    6. The annual budget is balanced and regularly monitored to avoid unanticipated deficits.
III. Physical Resources
    1. The collections are seen as a strategic resource that supports the museum's mission and vision.
    2. The collections are well organized, documented, and maintained, and they receive regular use by museum constituents.
    3. Special exhibitions generate community interest, attracting new and established audiences.
    4. The building and grounds are well maintained, and all systems are in good working order.
    5. The building and grounds enable the museum to realize its mission and advance its strategic plan.
IV. Community Support
    1. The museum is aware of and responsive to trends in the communities it serves.
    2. The museum's website and social media platforms extend its reach to real and virtual visitors.
    3. Outreach facilities and programs enable the museum to spread its mission into the community.
    4. The museum is seen as a valuable asset to the community.
    5. The museum has formed mutually beneficial relationships and partnerships with other community organizations.
    6. The museum has positive relationships with regional and national agencies that support arts and culture.
    7. The museum's audience reflects the community in which it exists.

enters their names and email addresses in the online app, they will be able to enter their responses, which will be tabulated, providing average scores for each statement and category. Their responses will be logged anonymously, but the app will show the administrator who has completed the survey and who needs a reminder.

When all the responses have been tallied, the administrator will share **Report 4: Institutional Audit Summary** with Search Committee members, suggesting that they may wish to print it out in preparation for the retreat.

Report 4: Institutional Audit Summary

In the report, each statement is scored numerically, ranging from a low of 1 to a high of 5. The template automatically calculates an average score for each statement and for the four categories of statements. This data can be viewed as a whole or by group (Board, Executive Committee, Staff, and Community Member).

Rather than focusing on specific numbers in detail, consider responses that receive ratings above 3.25 as positive. Scores below 3.25 suggest room for improvement. As you start analyzing the numbers, ask: Which of the four areas have the most positive responses? Which have the most negative responses?

An Example from a Hypothetical Museum

To analyze the sample data, begin by looking at figure 2.1, which shows average ratings for the individual statements and the four categories from all respondents to the survey. Scores for Financial Resources and Physical Resources fall in the positive area—above 3.7—while both Human Resources and Community Support are below 3.

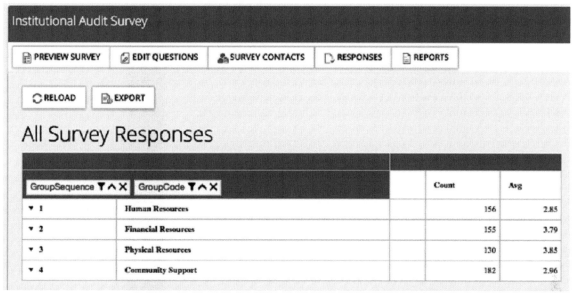

FIGURE 2.1
Institutional Audit Summary: Categories (Courtesy of the Museum Trustee Association)

With this big picture in mind, you can analyze the data further by looking at the scores for individual statements within each category. There were several low scores in the Human Resources category (figure 2.2). The low scores on statement 1 may be a reflection of a small staff running many time-intensive programs, but note the sharp discrepancy between the board rating of 2.20 and the staff and community (1.70 and 1.75, respectively). The high scores on statement 2 suggest that the new director will be inheriting a cohesive staff: the staff's average score was 4.0. The relatively low scores on statements 3, 4, and 5 about the board and statement 6 about the volunteer corps suggest that the new leader will need to be someone with demonstrated success in board and volunteer development.

Category	Seq	Question	Board Member Count	Board Member Avg	Community Count	Community Avg	Executive Commitee Count	Executive Commitee Avg	Staff Member Count	Staff Member Avg
Human Resources	1	The size and experience of the staff are adequate to fulfill the museum's mission.	5	2.20	8	1.75	3	2.33	10	1.70
	2	The staff has a positive attitude and works well as a team.	5	3.40	8	3.38	3	4.00	10	4.00
	3	The board has a clear understanding of its role in governing the museum annd the necessary experience and leadership to do so.	5	3.20	8	3.25	3	3.00	10	2.70
	4	The board, staff, and volunteer corps reflect the communities the museum aims to serve.	5	3.20	8	3.25	3	3.33	10	3.00
	5	The board and the staff have an effective working relationship.	5	3.20	8	3.25	3	3.33	10	3.00
	6	The museum has a knowledgeable and dependable volunteer corps.	5	2.40	8	2.00	3	2.67	10	2.10

FIGURE 2.2
Institutional Audit Summary: Human Resources, Responses by Group (Courtesy of the Museum Trustee Association)

The average score of 3.79 for Financial Resources (figure 2.3) identifies this as an area of strength on which the new director will build. The score of 4.23 on statement 4 suggests success in securing grants and private and corporate funding. Comparing this score with 3.46 on statement 1 and 3.36 on statement 2 suggests that the museum is more reliant on soft money than on regular sources of revenue, such as earned income and memberships. What implications does this have for the skills the Search Committee will seek in the museum's next leader?

				Count	Avg
▼ 2	▼ Financial Resources	▼ 1	Earned income generates appropriate support for the museum's facilities, operations, and programs.	26	3.46
		▼ 2	Museum membership provides a sustainable source of revenue and support.	25	3.36
		▼ 3	Board and development staff members work in concert to cultivate and grow the donor base.	26	4.27
		▼ 4	The museum is able to generate support for temporary exhibits and other special projects through grants, private, and corporate funding.	26	4.23
		▼ 5	The museum has an investment policy that generates appropriate returns to provide for the museum's current and future financial health.	26	3.92
		▼ 6	The annual budget is balanced and monitored regularly to avoid unanticipated deficits.	26	3.46
	Financial Resources Total			155	3.79

FIGURE 2.3
Institutional Audit Summary: Financial Resources, Responses by Question (Courtesy of the Museum Trustee Association)

Physical Resources also received high scores; however, the detailed report (figure 2.4) reveals a few troubling scores. Statements 2 and 3 about exhibitions and collections care both show a marked difference between the Executive Committee and the board, on the one hand, and staff, on the other. A high priority for the new director in this hypothetical museum would be making the board more familiar with those critical issues of the museum's operations. The community respondents gave relatively low ratings to statements 4 and 5 about the buildings and grounds. The museum might need to take a fresh look at its facilities and move those up on the priority list.

			Group ▼ ∧ X								
			Board Member		Community		Executive Committee		Staff Member		
Category ▼ ∧ X	Seq ▼ ∧ X	Question ▼ ∧ X	Count	Avg	Count	Avg	Count	Avg	Count	Avg	
▸ Human Resources			30	2.93	48	2.81	18	3.11	60	2.75	
▸ Financial Resources			30	3.70	48	3.79	18	3.83	59	3.81	
▼ Physical Resources	▼ 1	The collections are seen as a strategic resource that supports the museum's mission and vision.	5	4.60	8	4.25	3	4.67	10	4.60	
	▼ 2	The collections are well organized, documented, maintained, and receive regular use by museum constituents.	5	3.60	8	4.50	3	3.67	10	4.80	
	▼ 3	Special exhibitions generate community interest, attracting new and established audiences.	5	3.40	8	4.38	3	3.00	10	4.50	
	▼ 4	The building and grounds are well maintained and all systems are in good working order.	5	3.20	8	2.75	3	3.33	10	3.90	
	▼ 5	The building and grounds enable the museum to realize its mission and advance its strategic plan.	5	3.00	8	2.63	3	3.67	10	3.10	
Physical Resources Total			25	3.52	40	3.70	15	3.67	50	4.18	

FIGURE 2.4
Institutional Audit Summary: Physical Resources, Responses by Group (Courtesy of the Museum Trustee Association)

Community Support (figure 2.5) was also an area of weakness, with an overall category score of 2.96. Here again, the individual statements reveal strengths and areas of concern. The outlier is statement 6, on regional and national agencies, which received a score 4.31. Compared with the considerably lower scores on other statements, such as the 2.54 on statement 1 and 2.15 on statement 7, the audit suggests a need for a director who can make progress on community equity and access.

				Count	Avg
▼ 4	▼ Community Support	▼ 1	The museum is aware of and responsive to trends in the communities it serves.	26	2.54
		▼ 2	The museum's website and social media platforms extend its reach to real and virtual visitors.	26	2.92
		▼ 3	Outreach facilities and programs enable the museum to spread its mission into the community.	26	2.65
		▼ 4	The museum is seen as a valuable asset to the community.	26	3.69
		▼ 5	The museum has formed mutually beneficial relationships and partnerships with other community organizations.	26	2.42
		▼ 6	The museum has positive relationships with regional and national agencies that support arts and culture.	26	4.31
		▼ 7	The museum's audience reflects the community in which it exists.	26	2.15
	Community Support Total			182	2.96

FIGURE 2.5
Institutional Audit Summary: Community Support, Responses by Question (Courtesy of the Museum Trustee Association)

If significant challenges or divergent opinions are identified in the Institutional Audit, the Search Committee might benefit from the help of an outside facilitator who can review the data from the Institutional Audit, facilitate the Search Committee retreat, and debrief with the committee chair. A committee that decides to conduct its own retreat should also appoint a facilitator, preferably someone who is not a member of the Search Committee.

Template 5: Search Committee Retreat Guide

This template is designed as a guide for those who will facilitate and summarize the Search Committee retreat. It poses questions that will help the committee reflect on the data gathered in the survey, and then it explores the implications more deeply through the lenses of a SWOT analysis, a trend analysis, and an institutional life cycle model. The administrator will use this template to summarize the discussions, record the exercises, and analyze the feedback gathered at the retreat. This narrative snapshot of the museum at this moment in time will help the Search Committee think strategically about the next part of the search process—identifying the skills and qualities needed in the new leader.

Template 5: Search Committee Retreat Guide includes the names of those who attended, the date of the meeting, and the location. The administrator or a member of the Search Committee will record the highlights of the retreat, summarizing activities and discussions that focus attention on the museum's strengths, weaknesses, opportunities, and threats, as well as trends for the future and the museum's place in its institutional life cycle. (For a description of a SWOT Analysis and Institutional Life Cycle Model, see appendix C, pages 75–78.) This document will identify the big issues that the new director will need to address. In doing so, it will prepare the Search Committee to use **Template 6: Professional Skills and Personal Qualities** to prioritize what's needed in the new leader and to articulate the responsibilities and opportunities in **Template 7: Position Announcement**.

Although the **Search Committee Retreat Guide** is primarily an internal tool, an edited version of the highlights might be helpful in giving final candidates a sense of the opportunities and challenges they would face. It may also be the basis of performance objectives that will measure the new director's progress during the transition year.

External Perspectives

In addition to gathering internal perspectives, the Search Committee needs to know how the museum is perceived in the larger community at this important moment in its institutional development. To augment the responses to the Institutional Audit, Search Committee members should take responsibility for talking to selected funding agencies, community partners, and other stakeholders to assess the museum's reputation. To get their fingers on the pulse of the community, individual members of the Search Committee can also network within their own circles of acquaintances. Through one-on-one conversations, they can gather valuable qualitative data and write a short report to share with the committee at the retreat.

Questions they may want to address include:

- What do individuals and organizations perceive as the museum's mission and reason for being?
- Do many and varied community groups see the museum as a valuable asset? If so, what do they mention as its greatest strengths?
- What areas of improvement do they identify?
- How well does the museum collaborate with other community organizations?
- Do donors see it as an attractive institution to support?
- Do public and private schools see it as a valuable supplement to their curricula?
- Do diverse communities see the museum as a safe place to gather for meaningful discourse?
- What community values are embodied in the museum? What values are not evident?
- Is the museum a point of local or regional pride?

TEMPLATE 5: SEARCH COMMITTEE RETREAT GUIDE

Facilitator:

Participants:

Date:

Institutional Audit Survey Review

1. Which of the four categories (Human Resources, Financial Resources, Physical Resources, External Conditions) received the highest overall average?
   Discuss and note the implications for the new director search.

2. Which of the four categories received the lowest average?
   Discuss and note the implications for the new director search.

3. What are the biggest surprises?
   Note responses.

4. Looking at individual statements, which three statements received the highest average scores?

      1.

      2.

      3.

   These are the greatest strengths on which the new director will build.

5. Do these strengths fall into any one area, or are they spread throughout all four categories?
   Discuss and note the implications for the new director search.

6. Looking at the greatest strengths, are there any that could lead to weaknesses?
   Discuss and note the implications for the new director search.

7. Looking at individual statements, which three statements received the lowest average scores?

      1.

      2.

      3.

   These are the greatest challenges the new director must meet.

8. Do these challenges fall into any one area, or are they spread throughout all four categories?
   Discuss and note the implications for the new director search.

9. Looking at the most serious challenges, are there any that hold potential for positive growth?
   Discuss and note the implications for the new director search.

10. What is the relationship between the most serious challenges and the greatest strengths?
    Discuss and note the implications for the new director search.

11. Identify any areas where staff responses differ significantly from Search Committee responses. What does this suggest in terms of new leadership?
    Discuss and note the implications for the new director search.

SWOT Analysis

Review the SWOT description in appendix C, then consider the following. Some strengths and weaknesses are related; one may be the flipside of the other. Strengths and weaknesses are also a matter of degree. Too much of something—even a good thing—can distract an institution from its central mission.

12. What strengths and weaknesses are related?
    Discuss and note the implications for the new director search.

13. What do these suggest about the professional skills and personal qualities needed in the new director?
    Discuss and note the implications for the new director search.

14. What threats and opportunities are related?
    Discuss and note the implications for the new director search.

15. What do these suggest about the professional skills and personal qualities needed in the new director?
    Discuss and note the implications for the new director search.

Trends

Many threats present corresponding opportunities to respond to changing conditions in ways that will make the organization stronger. Look at issues and trends in the community and discuss the following questions:

16. What are the critical issues this year?
    Discuss and note the implications for the new director search.

17. What are they likely to be in three to five years?
    Discuss and note the implications for the new director search.

18. What old threats continue to concern us?
    Discuss and note the implications for the new director search.

19. What new threats have emerged during the past year?
    Discuss and note the implications for the new director search.

20. What opportunities exist now that didn't exist last year?
    Discuss and note the implications for the new director search.

21. List changes in the environment and prioritize in terms of impact.
    Discuss and note the implications for the new director search.

Institutional Life Cycle

Review the institutional life cycle in appendix C, and then answer the following questions:

22. In what stage of its institutional life cycle is the museum now?
    Discuss and note the implications for the new director search.

23. What does this suggest about the professional skills and personal qualities needed in a new director?
    Discuss and note the implications for the new director search.

NOTES

1. Diane Frankel, telephone interview with Daryl Fischer, July 21, 2017.

2. Ibid.

3. Kathryn R. Martin and Mary Baily Wieler, "Leadership Transitions: Move Forward, Be Confident—Be the Expert," Museum Trustee Association, April 29, 2016, accessed July 27, 2017, http://www.museumtrustee.org/tips-for-trustees/ leadership-transitions-move-forward-be-confident-be-the-expert.

3

The Search Stage

This phase of the executive transition involves many of the steps that boards typically identify with an executive search, but it is important to emphasize that it is the third stage of the process, not the first. Its success depends on the groundwork that has been laid.

During the Search Stage, the Search Committee will use five templates:

- **Template 6: Professional Skills and Personal Qualities** to identify and prioritize attributes needed in the new director
- **Template 7: Position Announcement** to articulate the opportunities of the position and the qualifications sought in the new leader
- **Template 8: Candidate Assessment Initial Review** to evaluate the initial pool of applicants
- **Templates 9A and B: Interview Outline/Skills and Qualities Assessment** to conduct interviews and select the top candidates
- **Template 10: Reference Check** to gather feedback from those who have known candidates

IDENTIFY AND RANK PROFESSIONAL SKILLS AND PERSONAL QUALITIES

By identifying the leadership skills, qualities, and experience needed to move the institution forward, the committee shifts its focus from the previous director's strengths or weaknesses to the museum's current and future needs. The goal is to neutralize past experiences (positive or negative) and start the search with a clean slate. This will maximize opportunities for growth and help the Search Committee to think strategically about how to transform this opening into an opportunity. If the outgoing director was much admired, it is especially important to realize that he or she cannot be cloned. Looking for a replacement with exactly the same skills, education, experience, and personality will lead to disappointment and may cause the committee to overlook other qualities that are more important for the museum's future. If the outgoing director was not highly respected, it is unwise to make his or her weaknesses the primary criteria for choosing a replacement. The committee must be proactive rather than reactive, focusing on what it is seeking rather than what it is replacing.

Combining objective and subjective qualities, the Search Committee will identify the background, skills, values, and work styles that are essential for the museum's continued health and growth at this particular moment in its life. Then it will be able to envision and describe the right candidate to fill the position. To do this, the committee should ask two questions:

- What most needs to change, and what kind of leader will it take to inspire these changes? If, for example, the museum needs to reinvent itself, it will be critical to find a director who is a blue-sky thinker and an innovator. If it needs to find new sources of revenue, it will benefit from someone with a bold, entrepreneurial spirit. If reaching out to broader audiences is a strategic priority, it must find someone with lived experiences that create a genuine understanding and appreciation of diverse perspectives.
- What are the deeply held values that must not change, and what kind of leader shares these values? If, for example, the museum is dedicated to serving youth and families, it would be critical to find someone who has demonstrated a commitment to young people. If the museum's mission is rooted in the sense of discovery, it would be important to find someone who has personally experienced the thrill of exploration and experimentation and wants to share it with others.

The Search Committee will need to consider many different aspects of candidates, ranging from clear-cut, objective characteristics to softer, more subjective traits. The factual issues—such as education, training, experience, skills, and capacities—are easier to assess, quantify, and compare across candidates. One of the committee's greatest challenges—and one of its most important contributions—is to determine the best fit between the vision and values of the institution and the vision and values of the candidates. This means focusing on subjective traits, such as core values, behaviors, attitudes, personalities, and work styles.

Template 6: Professional Skills and Personal Qualities

The Search Committee retreat clarifies the skills and experience needed in a new leader. With these insights, the committee is ready to rank specific skills and qualities, bringing the priorities for the search into sharper focus. This template, which lists a variety of professional skills and personal qualities, is a good starting point. It can be easily modified by the administrator to include other assets deemed important by the Search Committee.

Professional Skills	*Personal Qualities*
Fund development	Ability to inspire/empower others
Donor solicitation	Personal motivation
Corporate sponsorship	Ability to delegate
Grant writing	Visionary
Financial management	Articulate speaker
Facilities management	Good listener
Staff management	Good writer
Board relations	Appreciation of diverse perspectives
Strategic planning	Member of an important constituency
Membership development/retention	Team builder
Marketing/public relations	Problem solver
Knowledge of museum's discipline	Community minded
Professional networking	Change agent
National/international perspective	Visitor oriented
Education/interpretation	Flexible
Evaluation/audience research	Mature

Professional Skills	Personal Qualities
Programming/special events	Hands-on
Exhibition planning	Dynamic
Publications	Thoughtful/reflective
Technology	Ability to be self-reflective
Multidisciplinary perspective	Energetic
Volunteer management	Entrepreneurial
Community relations	Passionate about the museum's discipline
Social media	Imaginative
Community collaborations	Perceptive
Nonprofit leadership	Collaborative

Each professional skill can require different types of expertise depending on the museum's needs. The committee should be as specific as possible. If staff/volunteer management is a priority, will the new director need to set up new personnel management systems, assess the effectiveness of current systems, or build cross-departmental teams? If financial management is a priority, is it more important to know accounting procedures inside and out or how to manage endowment funds? If donor solicitation is a priority, will the new director need to raise money from corporate donors or cultivate relationships with private collectors?

When looking at personal qualities, the Search Committee's challenge is to consider each one in light of the museum's mission and the ability of the new director to advance that mission. What types of relationships are most critical with internal audiences, such as staff members, trustees, and volunteers? What relationships are most vital with external audiences, such as museum members, community organizations, and other institutions? What qualities would help to build and sustain mutually successful relationships with each of these constituencies?

The following exercise will help the Search Committee decide on the most essential skills and qualities—those that are either deal makers or deal breakers. For example, expertise in board relations would be essential in an institution that is making the shift from a founding board to a board that reflects the community. Listing the essential minimum requirements and the desirable options will help the committee to be concrete and focused.

1. Email the spreadsheet or distribute hard copies of **Template 6: Professional Skills and Personal Qualities** at a Search Committee meeting. Ask each member to rank each item on a scale of 1–3, with 1 being unimportant and 3 being essential, and then check the three most important skills and the three most important qualities in the third column.
2. Go around the room, listing everyone's "essential" (3 on the scale) skills on a flip chart labeled "Needed Professional Skills."
3. Then ask, "Are there any skills you rated 2 that you absolutely don't want to lose sight of before moving on?"
4. Repeat steps 2 and 3 with another flip chart labeled "Needed Personal Qualities."
5. When all skills and qualities have been listed, give each committee member four dots. Ask them to go to the flip chart and place two dots on the professional skills they believe will be most essential in the new director and two on the most crucial personal qualities.
6. Count the dots on each list to prioritize the five professional skills and the five personal qualities you will seek in your new director.

WRITE THE JOB DESCRIPTION

A well-written job description communicates the museum's expectations and inspires potential candidates. Action-oriented and tied to the museum's mission, the description outlines the director's role in realizing the mission. As long as it is well-conceived and comprehensive, the document can be brief or several pages long, depending upon the desired level of detail.

The job description should spell out everything potential candidates may want to know about the museum, from general responsibilities to specific tasks, and everything the Search Committee is looking for in a candidate, from educational background to professional experience. It should also describe the museum's resources and the board's expectations for the position. This multipurpose document will be useful in writing the position announcement, evaluating candidates, clarifying the responsibilities and expectations of the position, determining compensation, and evaluating the new director. It may also help in planning the new director's orientation and first-year transition.

The job description is a living document that should be read and referred to from time to time, not filed away. Although specific goals and objectives will evolve as the museum's strategic priorities shift, the job description provides the framework for the new director's roles and responsibilities.

The job description for the new leader will not necessarily look like the job description for the previous director. Although the committee may want to start by reviewing the existing job description, it should consider all of the following:

- *Current responsibilities.* If the current director is still on board or readily available, ask him or her to make a list of the most important duties and functions—both ongoing and intermittent. The Search Committee may also want to ask the board chair to list his or her regular interactions with the director. The common areas of responsibility might be included in the job description.
- *Future needs.* Refer to the museum's strategic plan to identify the museum's institutional goals and new initiatives. Consider special projects such as a new building, a capital campaign, or a major grant initiative.
- *Resources.* The new leader will have a role in managing existing resources and developing new resources that are needed in order to realize the museum's mission. Consider the human, physical, and financial resources identified in **Report 4: Institutional Audit Summary**.
- *Constituencies.* Museums cannot hope to be more successful in serving external audiences without serving internal audiences. Consider both constituencies and the new director's relationship with each.

The key elements are as follows:

- *Position title and classification* (if applicable). City and university museums are most likely to utilize a position classification system.
- *Reporting relationships.* If the director is responsible to multiple governing bodies, identify and describe the relationships. Indicate those staff positions that report directly to the director.
- *Mission* and *vision statements.* These foundational documents will be the basis for initial and ongoing conversations with candidates.
- *Description of the museum.* In addition to location, collection, programs and services, and building and grounds, be sure to include outreach facilities.
- *Financial resources.* Summarize the annual operating budget, sources of support—short-term and ongoing—and the director's annual fundraising responsibilities.

- *Human resources*. Provide the number of paid staff members (full-time and part-time) and volunteers, as well as their expertise.
- *General responsibilities*. For example, leading and motivating staff, expanding and diversifying audience, establishing and maintaining professional standards, guaranteeing the care of the collections, and ensuring the overall financial strength of the museum.
- *Specific responsibilities for current and upcoming projects*. For example, fundraising for building renovation with a cost estimated at $3.6 million.
- *Educational requirements*, minimum and desirable. If the Search Committee is seeking a candidate with diverse life experiences and perspectives, this is a place to demonstrate flexibility and creativity in weighing candidates' formal education background. Requiring advanced degrees can have the effect of limiting the applicant pool at this crucial stage of the search process.
- *Professional experience*, minimum and desirable. Here, again, new skill sets and perspectives may be every bit as valuable as traditional museum experience.
- *Relationships with key internal constituencies*, such as board, staff, volunteers, faculty, and students. Mention committees or councils on which the director typically serves.
- *Relationships with key external audiences*, such as community leaders, other cultural institutions, donors, members, the academic community, tribal representatives, and cultural tourists.
- *Salary*. This is a key factor for most prospective candidates, so at least provide a range and say commensurate with experience.
- *Benefits*. In addition to health insurance, retirement, life insurance, long-term disability, and professional development, some museums offer sabbaticals, cars, and housing allowances.

In short, the ideal job description is descriptive without being prescriptive. It should be as specific as possible in delineating the goals, resources, and standards of the museum without recommending the way to accomplish the goals, maximize the resources, or maintain the standards. It should not spell things out in such detail that candidates can simply tell the Search Committee what it wants to hear. Programming a person to carry out the board's initiatives does not give the new executive an opportunity to lead, and it may set him or her up for failure.

Posting the job description on your museum's website makes it accessible to anyone who wants to learn more about the position. An "Employment Opportunities" button on the home page can lead candidates to download the job description. Or insert a single-line notice of the position on the home page and link it to an email form or a download. However the posting is accessed, make sure to note that the museum is an equal opportunity employer.

DEVELOP THE COMPENSATION PACKAGE
The Search Committee should work in concert with the Personnel Committee to develop the compensation package. Although the salary of the previous director may be a useful starting point, it is important to review current salary scales for directors of similar institutions. Executive compensation data are readily available today. Regional museum associations and other professional networks, such as the Association of Art Museum Directors, publish salary surveys of their members.[1] The salaries of directors of individual museums are matters of public record, filed on IRS Form 990 and available online at Guidestar.org (see **Resource Guide**). To attract qualified candidates, especially those who would need to relocate, the salary offered should be at least mid-range for the type of museum, annual budget, and geographic area. As leaders of nonprofit institutions, boards should make every effort to compensate for gender bias in executive salaries. Once the salary range is identified, it is included in the position announcement, along with employer-paid benefits, such as pension and life, health, and disability insurances.

In addition to financial remuneration, the announcement should include nonfinancial benefits, such as vacation time, flexible scheduling, and relocation allowance. In budgeting for the new director's salary, the Executive, Personnel, and Finance Committees should all weigh in on the long-term implications for the budget. Is the institution able to fund that level of compensation for an extended period, or will the director be expected to raise additional funds to support his or her salary? If this is the case, this assumption must be communicated clearly.

ARTICULATE THE POSITION

Template 7: Position Announcement

Writing the position announcement is one of the most challenging and important steps in the search stage because it determines the initial pool of applicants—whether in small- to medium-sized museums that are conducting their own searches or in large museums with human resource departments. **Template 7: Position Announcement** is geared toward potential candidates as well as those who can put the Search Committee in touch with candidates. Its purpose is to attract candidates by describing the institution and the position broadly but articulately and strategically in terms that are relevant and interesting to prospective candidates. The Search Committee must think in terms of not only what it's "buying" but also what it's "selling"—the museum and the community. Later, interested candidates will receive more detailed information, but the importance of achieving the right tone in the position announcement cannot be overemphasized. As in personal introductions, there's only one opportunity to make a first impression.

The position announcement should attract the attention of candidates, inspire them to consider the position and learn more about it, and explain how and when to submit the necessary application materials. If the job description is posted on the museum's website, the position announcement should include the URL where candidates can find it.

Generally, position announcements can accomplish everything they need to in 350–500 words. Extra words may give the impression that the museum is not clear about its priorities. Honing the announcement down to its essence takes time, but it pays off by communicating a clear and positive image of the museum.

Keep these basic rules in mind when writing the announcement:

- Write from the perspective of the candidate, not from the perspective of the board, the Search Committee, or the institution. What would a candidate want to know about the museum, the position, and the community? What makes the position particularly challenging, stimulating, or exciting?
- Focus on mission and vision, not simply responsibilities and requirements. Nonprofit executive directors rank mission as the single most important factor in their decisions to take their current jobs, but, surprisingly, not all position announcements even mention mission.
- Catch readers' attention by starting with a headline that will make them want to read further. Communicate the most compelling reasons for working at your museum—clearly and early in the announcement. Since people will be reading your job posting along with dozens of others, consider what would make it stand out in the minds of the serious searcher and the casual browser.

Here's how a new museum emphasized the groundbreaking nature of its leadership potential: "This is a unique opportunity to shape a new museum and be part of the downtown renaissance of one of America's fastest-growing cities. Innovative and unexpected programming in three off-site 'galleries' will extend the museum into the urban landscape and expand the realm of public art."

Many position announcements are weighted toward either describing the institution or describing the ideal candidate. **Template 7: Position Announcement** suggests how to achieve a balance and can be easily tailored to

TEMPLATE 7: POSITION ANNOUNCEMENT

{[Museum Name]}

Executive Director [or other title]

Position Headline [phrase to distinguish this from other similar positions]

The {[Museum Name]} is a [type] museum known for its collection of [collection area(s)]. Less known, but equally noteworthy, is our [other collection areas, outreach facilities, etc.]. The museum is located in [name of city], a [city, town, metropolitan area, rural area] of [population] that is home to [identify primary industries and attractions].

The {[Museum Name]} seeks a [insert adjectives from Personal Skills list] to help realize our mission of "{[Mission Statement]}" and advance our strategic goals of [insert strategic priorities]. With support from [source], the museum has engaged in [insert name of initiative] that aims to [insert intended outcomes]. Partnerships have been formed with [names of organizations/institutions], which share our goals of [insert]. [If the museum is engaged in a capital campaign or building project, include here.]

The museum was founded in [year] by [individual or group] with the goal of [insert verbiage from founding charter]. It is housed in [identify building sizes and types] located on [describe physical surroundings]. With a staff of [number] full-time, [number] part-time, and [number] volunteers, and a board of [number], the museum serves [number] visitors annually, drawing from [describe area or region]. [Insert program names] are well-established programs that have a loyal following. We are attracting and serving new audiences with [insert program names].

The [budget number] annual budget is supplemented by [number] dollars of support from [name], a [local/state/regional] [foundation/agency]. In addition, [insert name], an annual fundraiser, generates approximately [number] dollars. The {[Museum Name]} currently has a [number of months/years] grant from [agency] to involve [target audience(s)] in [insert intended outcomes].

The director is charged with managing [identify area(s)], implementing [identify area(s)], envisioning [identify area(s)], and strengthening [identify area(s)]. The successful candidate will be able to [verb], [verb], and [verb] staff, board, and volunteers and [verb] and [verb] the museum's external stakeholders. He or she will have demonstrated experience in [insert from Professional Skills list] and a strong background in [discipline or skill set]. An equal opportunity employer, the {[Museum Name]} is seeking candidates with [number] years of [identify] experience and [bachelor's/master's/PhD] in [discipline(s)]; it will also consider those who have other valuable experience and perspectives to bring to bear. Competitive salary and attractive benefits package. To be considered for this [insert adjectives] position, please submit [letter of interest/resume/references] by [date].

[Contact name]

[Address]

[City/State/Zip code]

[Email address]

the specifics of your museum by filling in the bracketed areas with specific information. Some committees will find this format helpful; others will prefer to take a do-it-yourself approach. If you write your own position announcement, you may still choose to print the template and use it as a guide. In either case, give thoughtful consideration to the following:

- Describe your institution in terms that will attract the attention of candidates and answer their questions. Use descriptive adjectives, such as *innovative, historic, imaginative, unique, growing,* or *public/private* in summarizing the museum's past and future.
- Promote the location as well as the institution, describing the population, natural resources, industries, and educational institutions in your area.
- State (or summarize) your museum's mission statement and vision statement, if applicable. Then mention ways in which your museum is achieving its mission, such as new initiatives or strategic alliances.
- Describe the responsibilities of the position, using active verbs and nouns, such as *manage, lead, implement, envision, initiate, ensure, strengthen,* and *leverage.*
- Describe the person you are seeking. Borrow language from **Template 6: Professional Skills and Personal Qualities**, including descriptive words from the list of personal qualities and skill sets from the list of professional skills.
- Summarize the museum's organizational structure, including whether it is a separate 501(c)(3) or a department of a larger entity and to whom the director reports.
- Mention the salary and benefits—a range or a general statement. For many candidates, this is a key factor in whether to consider a position (especially if it involves relocation), so be as specific as possible.
- Outline the application procedures, including application deadline and anticipated starting date for the position.

ANNOUNCE THE POSITION

When announcing the position, the Search Committee must first decide on the scope of the search. Where you cast your net will determine what you catch. These days, most museums commit to at least a regional search with the potential to expand it nationally. There is nothing to lose and much to gain by getting the word out as broadly as possible. There are four principal avenues: advertising, sourcing, word-of-mouth, and conferences.

Today, advertising on the web has become the norm because of the advantages to those on both sides of the job search. For candidates, websites provide constantly updated job postings, links to other job search sites, career development tips, and other resources. For search committees, websites are an efficient and economical way to reach thousands of candidates. Many websites can track the response to your ad. Posting a job electronically is easy. You can submit your position announcement in the body of an email or attach it as a Word or PDF document. Include the museum's website and your museum logo, if possible. Fees vary with different organizations, ranging from a low of $100 to a high of $350 for a thirty-day posting for member institutions. Non-member rates are higher, ranging from $200 to $550 for thirty-day postings. For an additional fee, some sites offer feature ads that include a display ad in the organization's magazine or a listing in their e-newsletter. Some of the best options are:

- Major professional organizations have online job boards, such as the American Alliance of Museums' online JobHQ and the Association of Children's Museums' classifieds.
- Discipline-specific organizations, such as the College Art Association's career center, the Association of Academic Museums and Galleries' job postings, the American Association for State and Local History's career center, and the Association of Science-Technology Centers' job bank are good ways to target your search.

- State and regional museum association websites also include job boards. Postings are typically free for member institutions, and rates range from $50 to $100 for non-members. State associations generally only post jobs within the state, so regional associations are a good way to cast a wider net.

Many position announcements include a statement about being an equal opportunity employer, but the reality is that in 2014 only 7 percent of nonprofit CEOs were people of color.[2] To go beyond the boilerplate of an affirmative action policy, search committees should be intentional about seeking out networks that will reach a diverse pool of candidates, such as:

- The American Alliance of Museums Professional Networks such as Asian Pacific American, DIVCOM (diversity and inclusion), Indigenous Peoples Museum Network, Latino, and LGBTQ Alliance
- New organizations, such as Museum Hue, that attract and serve job seekers with diverse backgrounds
- Philanthropic and leadership projects focused on diversity and inclusion, such as the Association of Black Foundation Executives, the Philanthropic Initiative for Racial Equity, the Aspen Institute, the New American Leaders Project, and the Jamestown Project
- Professional women's groups, such as ArtTable, a national nonprofit network of 1,200 women leaders in the visual arts

Advertising in print media is a traditional way of seeking candidates that is still used by some museums, especially those with national reputations and large budgets. Many publications offer a combined price for a print ad and an electronic posting. Consider the following:

- The *Chronicle of Philanthropy* is read by many museum professionals, especially directors.
- Sunday newspapers in major metropolitan areas are likely to have a diverse community of candidates who would be interested in museum careers.
- If you're intentionally seeking a director with experience in a particular field, research the discipline-specific publications she or he is likely to be reading.

Tailor your position announcement to the publication's readers. An ad on AAM's JobHQ would not be appropriate for a newspaper, which has a much broader readership. If the museum is not well known, list a couple of noteworthy facts, and be sure to speak to the mission.

The **Resource Guide** at the back of this book lists websites that museum directors are likely to read. With the ever-growing number of options, it is worthwhile to do some surfing yourself. If you find the content useful, the chances are good that the candidates you are seeking will too. In addition to content, clear organization and easy navigation are features that will attract candidates and bring them back.

Word of mouth is always a productive way to spread the word about positions in the museum field. The Search Committee should ask staff members, fellow trustees, and colleagues in other nonprofit institutions to let others know about the position. Encourage them to post the position on free job boards or list serves they may be familiar with or to suggest places to put paid listings.

The Search Committee can also be more proactive by networking with colleagues locally and nationally, what search consultants refer to as "sourcing." Think about the circles in which the person you're looking for is likely to travel and work those networks through phone calls and emails. While these requests generally start with "Can you think of possible candidates?" a clear subtext is "Might you be interested in this position?" Ask for contact information of people the sources recommend whenever possible; do not rely on them to forward the posting to promising individuals. Encourage contacts to continue to think about candidates and get back to you with further ideas. After the call, send a thank-you email, reinforcing that message and encouraging them to share the posting within their networks.

Case in point: For one museum, networking was the key to success. The board enlisted the help of a retired director, who sent letters to many of her colleagues describing the position from her perspective and asking whether they knew anyone who might be interested. Through the grapevine, she heard of someone who was interested and contacted him. She acted as the liaison between the Search Committee and the candidate, who was eventually hired. Without the former director's connections, the committee and the new director would not have found each other.

Conferences can help you reach both serious job seekers and casual candidates. By attending regional and national museum conferences, committee members can put their fingers on the pulse of the museum community, learn about the big issues, and find out what comparable positions are available. They can review resumes and meet with prospective candidates in job placement centers, reporting back to the Search Committee on promising leads. Committee members should take copies of the job description and position announcement, as well as exhibition catalogues, newsletters, and brochures to share with potential candidates. Different conferences attract different types of delegates so consider "alternative" conferences like Museum Next or special-focus conferences, such as Museums and the Web.

CONSIDER INTERNAL CANDIDATES

The Search Committee must make it clear that the executive search is open to internal candidates. While current staff members require great sensitivity in the search process, they can also offer valuable benefits to an institution in transition:

- They understand the museum, its culture, and its history.
- They are loyal to the institution.
- They have already established relationships with many of the internal and external constituencies.
- They speak the language and share the values of the institution.
- They present fewer unknowns than external candidates.

The museum may have an institutional culture that supports the cultivation of leadership and promotion from within. Nevertheless, internal candidates often face obstacles in being chosen for positions of leadership. Internal promotions at the director's level are unusual in museums, so candidates must often move to another institution in order to advance. There are several reasons for this situation:

- Although everyone has strengths and weaknesses, the flaws of internal candidates are better known than the flaws of external candidates.
- Outsiders are more likely to be respected and viewed as experts.
- Search Committee members who know internal candidates in specific positions may have difficulty imagining the potential for transferable skills.
- Someone new often has more appeal to a Search Committee. However, new is not necessarily better when it comes to staff members with a proven track record.

If the Search Committee identifies any internal candidates as serious contenders, there are several important guidelines to follow. First and foremost, the names of staff candidates, like those of all candidates, should be held in complete confidence. They should never be revealed to the public or the rest of the staff.

Give internal candidates the same treatment and consideration as external candidates. When candidates are brought in from out of town, they are likely to have opportunities to get to know a variety of internal audiences through social interactions such as cocktails with board members or lunch with community members. Try to create the same kinds of opportunities for internal candidates. Don't just give them a two-hour interview and send them back to their desks. Plan for their interview in the same way you would plan for an out-of-town candidate.

Make it clear from the beginning whether the Search Committee is inclined to search vigorously for candidates outside the museum. If external candidates clearly have the edge, tell the internal candidates as soon as possible. Stringing them along to avoid eventual disappointment is worse than telling them up front that they are not being considered as seriously as external candidates.

If a board member wishes to be considered for the position, he or she should resign from the board to avoid a conflict of interest. If the board member is not selected and wishes to rejoin the board, he or she must go through the traditional nominating process. The board chair should talk candidly with the returning board member to ensure that he or she will be able to work with the new director.

ASSESS THE CANDIDATES

Template 8: Candidate Assessment

The initial review of applications provides an opportunity to measure first impressions and assess how candidates communicate in writing. Letters of inquiry, cover letters, expressions of interest, and questions about the position can reveal a lot about candidates. So can social media, so be sure to look at candidates' Facebook pages, LinkedIn profiles, Twitter accounts, and blogs. The entire Search Committee will review all applications using **Template 8: Candidate Assessment Initial Review**. That worksheet uses the top five professional skills and personal qualities identified in **Template 6: Professional Skills and Personal Qualities** as criteria for ranking applicants during the initial application review. This tool is also useful as a sorting device during the subsequent screening of the candidate pool—probably through the selection of the top three to five candidates. Although the committee may wish to refer to this template throughout the search process, it will be most useful in the early stages when the committee starts looking at applications and makes its first round of decisions. It is a tool to help committee members stay focused on the skills and qualities they identified as priorities when they might become distracted by extraneous information on candidates' applications.

After inserting the top five Professional Skills and Personal Qualities in the column headings according to the instructions in the online Help Manual, the administrator will send a link to each committee member with the date by which the assessment needs to be completed. In this case, it's important that each person includes his or her name to ensure full participation of the Search Committee. Committee members will use this form to rate each candidate in each of the ten categories on a scale of 1–4 (1 being poor, 4 being excellent). They can also note special considerations in the fourth column. Quantitative responses will be automatically tabulated, giving an average score for each candidate. In addition, the administrator will record any notes on the Initial Review Summary worksheet.

The template has spaces for thirty candidates. If the pool is exceptionally large, appoint a group of three or four members of the Search Committee to read all applications and sort out those that definitely do not meet the requirements for one reason or another.

Those candidates with the highest average scores warrant serious consideration, but it bears mentioning that these scores are a starting point, not the end point, in the process of narrowing the search pool to final candidates.

An Example from a Hypothetical Search Committee

The committee should look closely at the rankings before screening candidates further. For example, the sample **Candidate Assessment** (figure 3.1) indicates that Roosevelt, who has the highest overall score (365), did not have high scores in some of the skills and qualities identified by the committee as priorities. He had very high scores in Community Relations, Community Minded, Entrepreneurial, and Appreciation of Diverse Perspectives. In general, he scored higher in Personal Qualities than in Professional Skills, suggesting that interpersonal skills are his forte. If committee members decide to interview this candidate, they will need to assess his ability to learn new skills, which they might discover in the reference check by asking his references whether he is a quick study.

Considering the time and resources available, the Search Committee should choose between five and ten candidates at this stage. This is the first step in the screening process. These candidates will be sent information packets and contacted for phone interviews that will help to narrow the pool further. Candidates who are not selected will receive a letter thanking them for their interest.

From this point forward, the Search Committee will take a more qualitative approach to the review and selection process. It will assess candidates based primarily on their answers to interview questions, written material, and feedback gathered from reference checks. Committee members may want to refer back to the lists of skills and qualities in **Template 6: Professional Skills and Personal Qualities** to refocus their priorities during the interview, but in all likelihood, only candidates who have measured up to the criteria identified in that template will become

Greenville Museum of Art and History

Template 8: Candidate Assessment Initial Review
Total of all reviewers' scores
10 reviewers; maximum 40 points per skill or quality

Committee members graded each candidate on a scale of 1 to 4, 1 being poor and 4 being excellent on each of the skills and qualities.
Up to 4 extra points may be added for additional attributes noted in the Comments column.

Candidate Name	Skills					Qualities					Extra points	Comments	Total score
	Strategic planning	Donor solicitation	Staff management	Community relations	Board relations	Vision	Community minded	Team builder	Appreciation of diverse perspectives	Entrepreneurial			
Linda	22	26	27	26	22	31	22	31	22	26			255
Verne	22	22	26	37	26	37	26	26	22	22			266
Margaret	27	31	23	27	31	23	27	31	23	27			270
Les	32	22	27	32	23	36	31	27	27	31			288
Steve	27	27	31	32	31	27	32	31	31	27			296
Amanda	31	35	35	27	36	27	31	27	27	35	3	former staff member; former staff; knows us well	314
Madison	40	30	27	31	32	32	31	27	31	35			316
Emilio	27	27	31	40	27	27	40	31	40	27	7	lifelong Greenville resident; local!	324
Ellis	22	37	32	32	40	37	37	40	25	27			329
Andreas	27	40	37	32	31	35	35	32	33	27			329
Dan	31	32	31	40	27	35	36	36	32	32			332
Gail	27	33	35	40	32	40	36	33	27	31			334
Janeen	36	27	36	31	32	36	31	40	35	30			334
Jacqueline	32	31	40	40	36	31	35	35	40	27	2	doctoral thesis topic close to collections strength	349
Roosevelt	31	31	31	40	36	31	40	36	40	40	9	lifelong Greenville resident; also local; well respected in town	365

FIGURE 3.1
Candidate Assessment Initial Review (Courtesy of the Museum Trustee Association)

finalists. In the end, Search Committee members need to trust their judgment in making their final assessments. They were chosen for their perspective and expertise; these intrinsic qualities will be more useful than any tool.

RESPOND TO CANDIDATES

Email or call the candidates identified during the application review to express the Search Committee's interest in talking with them. Follow up with a packet of information (both online and hard copy) about the museum, including current exhibitions and programs, the annual budget, and the strategic plan to help candidates prepare for the initial interview. In the email, explain that a member of the Search Committee will be calling to schedule a preliminary phone interview and ask when would be the most convenient time to call.

It is not necessary to ask for references or salary history at this point. Many candidates don't appreciate being asked to provide such information until they have gotten to know more about the museum and have learned whether they are, indeed, a final candidate. Just as in personal relationships, it makes sense to establish a relationship first, decide whether you want to continue it, and, if so, move forward cautiously.

Assign a few committee members to call the five to ten candidates you want to pursue for a brief (fifteen- to twenty-minute) initial interview. We suggest reviewing the list of questions in **Template 9A: Interview Outline** and choosing a few introductory questions for all callers to ask. Gathering different perspectives on the candidates will be helpful, but so is a degree of consistency. A simple phone interview summary will ensure that everyone is posing the same questions in the same order and gathering the same preliminary information. It helps to take notes in real time and review after each call. Then share phone interview summaries with the committee before a meeting to narrow the candidate pool further by selecting a short list of three to six final candidates who will be invited for interviews.

The size of the interview pool is important. If it is either too large or too small, it will be harder to reach an appropriate decision. When in doubt about whether to bring in a candidate from out of town, the Search Committee should consider the cost of a plane ticket and a night in a hotel relative to the investment it will be making in hiring someone ($300,000 per year for an average of four to five years is $1.5 million!).

Case in point: In the interests of time and money, one museum decided to interview only two candidates. This decision turned out to be shortsighted because the committee wound up comparing two people whose personalities were so different that their personal styles became the issue rather than their individual skills and qualities. If a third person had been interviewed, the Search Committee might have been able to mitigate those differences or refocus on what factors were most important to the institution.

INTERVIEW FINAL CANDIDATES

Template 9A: Interview Outline

Round 1: Committee Phone Interviews

A conference call—preferably a videoconference—is the first opportunity for the entire Search Committee and the candidates to get to know one another, learning everything they need to know to make the right decision. To lay the proper foundation, the committee should create a climate that fosters frankness on both sides of the table. Making each candidate feel comfortable will elicit the maximum amount of information for the committee and the candidate.

Template 9A: Interview Outline lists suggested questions the Search Committee can ask to assess the candidates' responses and identify the best choice for the position. You won't want to ask every question on this list, and you may well want to add some of your own. The more your questions are tailored to the specific candidate and to the museum's culture, the more useful the interview will be. So give careful thought to selecting the most appropriate questions from the template; deleting those that are unnecessary, redundant, or inappropriate; and adding new questions as needed.

TEMPLATE 9A: INTERVIEW OUTLINE

Candidate's name:

Search committee members participating in this interview:

Please note if this is the

☐ First Interview or ☐ Second Interview

Interview date:

The Search Committee can draw from this list of questions for the first (video conference) and second (on-site) interviews with candidates. In each case, select questions from each of the following areas, assigning them to members of the committee so the same person poses the same questions to each candidate.

Introduction

What was it that interested you in this position?

What did you know about the museum before you applied for the position?

What were you most surprised to learn?

From what you have learned, what do you see as the museum's greatest assets? What do see as its greatest liabilities?

What are your first impressions of our city (positive and negative)?

Background

Please describe your personal interest in [insert the museum's discipline and/or area of special focus].

How did you get into the museum field?

What do you think are the most interesting new developments in [insert the museum's discipline and/or area of special focus] and museums in general?

Tell us about two programs or projects you've worked on that have given you the greatest satisfaction. Why did you choose these?

Now tell us about two programs or projects that have been your biggest disappointments. What did you learn from these?

Leadership

What are your deepest values and how do they fit with this position?

The new director will be the hub of a wheel that includes a [insert number] member board of trustees, a staff of [insert number], a volunteer corps of [insert number], and [insert description] community groups. Please describe your leadership style and tell us how you would tailor it each group.

What are the things that motivate you personally? How do you use these things to motivate others?

There are so many options for communicating these days—email, social media, one-on-one phone calls, conference calls, video conferencing, face-to-face meetings. Please describe your communication style and what options you favor.

What kind of a relationship would you like to have with staff? What would you do to cultivate that relationship?

What kind of relationship would you like to have with the board? What would you do to cultivate that relationship?

Strategic planning is an activity that boards and directors undertake periodically. What are your thoughts about thinking and acting strategically on an ongoing basis?

What is your approach to setting goals and monitoring performance?

Describe a situation where you felt strongly about a situation and encountered opposition. How did you resolve the issues?

Staff and Volunteer Management

How do you work with staff members at your current institution? Please give examples.

What do you consider the most important characteristics of a senior management team and how have you cultivated effective teamwork at that level?

What have you found to be the most effective way of motivating staff and volunteers? Give an example of how this practice has worked.

How do you promote understanding and cooperation between staff and volunteers?

How would your subordinates and colleagues describe your management style?

Other than specific job requirements and experience, what kind of characteristics do you look for in hiring new staff members?

Describe a difficult personnel situation you've handled. Tell us what happened, how it was resolved, and what you learned from it.

How have you rewarded exceptional performance?

What has been your most valuable professional development opportunity?

Financial Management

In your opinion, what kind of reporting structure is necessary to guarantee sound fiscal management?

Here is an example of the financial statement from [insert period]. What is most remarkable about this, and what does it suggest to you?

Under what circumstances are you comfortable incurring debt?

How would you manage an organization that is in debt?

What do you see as the optimum level of fund balance, and what are reasonable means to achieve this level?

What kinds of relationships do you cultivate with companies that provide goods and services to the museum?

Resource Development

Tell us about your most and least successful fundraising experiences and what you learned from each.

Where does friend raising fit into the scheme of resource development?

The museum currently has [insert number] members. This represents an [insert increase or decrease] of [insert percentage] over last year's membership. What would be your goals for membership, and how would you accomplish them?

The museum currently has an annual fund of [insert dollar amount]. This represents an [insert increase or decrease] of [insert percentage] over last year's annual fund. What would be your goals for growing/sustaining the annual fund, and how would you accomplish them?

What are the most important ingredients in a successful grant application?

What place should grant funding have in the overall organizational budget?

Reflecting on grants you've administered, what have been the greatest challenges and how have you met them?

Reflecting on grants you've administered, what have been the greatest opportunities and how have you maximized them?

Collections Management

You've seen a copy of our collections plan. Does this provide clear guidelines for acquisitions and deaccessions? If not, how would you change it?

Our acquisitions budget is $ [insert figure from designated funds, operations budget and fund-raisers]. How can we make the most of these dollars in today's collecting climate?

What is the appropriate place of long-term loans and promised gifts in the collections plan?

Approximately [insert number] percent of our collection is on view. What are your thoughts about the best ways of maximizing the reamining [insert number] percent that is in storage?

What are your thoughts and experience on using technology to make collections more accessible?

Programs

You've seen a list of our current programs. What criteria do you use to measure the success of programs and decide whether to continue them in the future?

During the past year our staff has [insert increased or decreased] by [insert number] percent and our programs have [insert increased or decreased] by [insert number] percent. Should this trend continue? If not, how would you reverse it?

Tell us about one of your most successful collaborations. What did you learn from it?

Now tell us about one of your least successful collaborations. What did you learn from it?

Facilities

This facility affords many advantages as well as some challenges including [insert challenges]. Based on your experience in managing facilities, how would you approach these?

External Relationships

What community-oriented values would you bring to the position?

What are your thoughts on a museum's role as a civic institution?

Considering the variety of community organizations on a scale of 1–10 (1 being extremely introverted, and 10 being extremely extroverted), where should the museum fall? What would you do to accomplish this?

How could we make the museum a source of pride for the many communities within our community?

What has been your involvement in professional organizations and how would you like to contribute to the profession going forward?

Analysis of Museum's Current Situation

Based on the information you've received about the museum, what do you see as the major challenges on the horizon?

Please choose one of the following issues [insert several issues identified in the Institutional Audit] that you think is central to the future of the museum and tell us how you would approach it.

Given the museum's current situation, how would you envision spending the majority of your time?

Personal

Please tell us four adjectives that describe you.

What are the greatest joys and frustrations of your current position?

What type of pressures do you feel in your current position? How do you cope with them?

What strategies do you use to deal with the multiple demands and regular interruptions that come with leadership?

What work environment best suits your style and why?

In your own estimation what are your chief weaknesses? How do you counteract, overcome, or accommodate them?

What kind(s) of opportunities would you like to have for professional growth?

Conclusion

Is there something you wish we'd asked you?

Are there any questions you'd like to ask of the Search Committee?

Once the questions have been chosen, the administrator should add museum-specific information. Print the revised Interview Outline and distribute it to the committee. The administrator can increase the spacing on this form to provide space for notes on each candidate's responses.

Try to schedule the phone interviews as close together as possible, ideally on consecutive days. For the committee, a compressed schedule will help in decision-making by bringing uniformity to the interviews and facilitating comparisons of candidates. For the final candidates, it will prevent a lengthy process. And for the staff, it will hasten a quick resolution to a long-awaited decision. If the interviews must be spread out for scheduling reasons, be sure to keep all candidates updated.

Unless they are human resources professionals or managers, most Search Committee members probably are not skilled interviewers. Before any candidate sits down at the table, be sure the members have been briefed on some basic rules. Don't assume that they know what to ask the candidate or how to phrase questions. Make it clear exactly what is appropriate, what is inappropriate, what is legal, and what is illegal. Questions about family background, lifestyle, and family relationships may seem innocent enough. But if they are inappropriate or illegal, they can not only make the candidate uncomfortable but also put the museum in jeopardy.

Candidates are likely to reveal many things about themselves in an interview. They are also liable to distort some things in order to be perceived favorably. Most search committees base their decisions on what candidates say about themselves and whatever can be gleaned from their resumes. Creating opportunities to see how each candidate approaches a problem provides a significant added edge. Each final candidate will have received background information about the museum, such as the strategic plan and financial reports. Ask them to tell you what they see as the major challenges and how they would spend the majority of their time. Or suggest a couple of topics for the interview, such as the financial health of the museum or the museum's place in the community. See which one they pick and how they approach the issue. Do they have all the answers, or do they ask questions to learn more?

This approach has several benefits. It will give you a truer glimpse into a candidate's approach and values in action. It will focus everyone on the mission of the museum and the needs of the community. It will make the interview more like a dialogue between the committee and the candidate than a one-way communication in which the committee poses all of the questions to the candidate. This approach is not unlike the request for proposals model used in selecting architects for a building project. After presenting a basic program, budget, and timeline, the building committee asks finalists to develop a conceptual design and uses that as the basis for their selection.

While allowing for individual differences to emerge, it is also important to create uniformity in the interviews. To facilitate sound decision-making, the Search Committee needs a way of looking at all candidates through the same lens and ranking them on the same scale. Develop some questions that will be asked of all candidates and group them into categories such as financial management, resource development, staff and volunteer management, leadership, and external relationships. Then assign questions to different committee members. You may want to start the interviews by asking candidates to say something about themselves, such as what interested them in this position. Ask them to prepare for an opening question such as "What do you see as the greatest impact museums can make today?" or "What prepares you for *this* job in *this* community?"

In addition to assigning the Search Committee's questions, some committees anticipate the questions they expect to get from candidates and assign committee members to prepare a response. When both the museum and the candidate are fully prepared for two-way questions, the interview will be more productive for both parties.

Demonstrating a high level of organization and preparedness is essential because the candidates are not the only ones who are being assessed during the interview. To reach a decision that is right for both parties, the committee must present an objective and accurate picture of the museum. This means revealing the extent of the challenges the museum faces as well as the opportunities. The director of a nonprofit support center says that one of the most common complaints from new directors is that the depth of financial problems or the level of staff conflict were not communicated clearly during their interviews.[3]

After thanking each candidate, allow a few minutes for committee members to record their impressions while they are still fresh in their minds. Since everyone will have observed different things, encourage them to share their initial reactions with one another. Further reflection sometimes yields valuable insights, so invite committee members to call or email the chair with additional thoughts about the candidates.

Template 9B: Skills and Qualities Assessment is a form (not illustrated) where committee members will rank each candidate on the top five Professional Skills and Personal Qualities that were identified in **Template 6: Professional Skills and Personal Qualities**. They will turn in their completed forms to the administrator, who will tabulate the responses.

Sometimes there is a high degree of consensus within the Search Committee. At other times, reactions are all over the map. Getting a reading on the committee's thinking will help the chair plan for the next step—choosing the finalist(s). You may want to try taking a straw vote, emphasizing to members that their responses are strictly for planning purposes, not for final decision-making.

Comparing the candidates' values with the museum's values is another useful technique. For each candidate, make a chart like the one below. On the left side, write a few words that summarize the museum's intrinsic values and its vision for the future. On the right side, write a few words that sum up the values and vision expressed by each candidate. Compare the words on each side. Draw lines connecting those that seem congruent; the more lines connecting the two lists, the better. Do any words seem to oppose one another? If so, this would be a red flag for the committee, suggesting that the museum's and the candidate's values may be incongruent.

Museum's Values	*Candidate's Values*
Community centered	Staff empowerment
Audience engagement	Community activist
Hub for innovation	Social justice
Racial equity and inclusion	Experimentation

If there is not clear consensus after the last candidate's interview, Search Committee members may need a little more time to reflect on each of the candidates. Everyone is always eager to identify a final candidate and move on with the transition, but, considering the importance of the decision, it is worth allowing a few extra days for committee members to reflect on their impressions of each candidate and see whether their initial impressions change one way or the other. Only once they've reached consensus about which candidates to invite for an onsite interview can the Search Committee move forward to the next step.

Round 2: In-person Interview

Planning the face-to-face interview requires two mind-sets: what the Search Committee needs to learn about the candidates, and what candidates need to learn about the opportunity and the community. At this stage of the process, everyone is eager to build relationships with candidates, but it can't be rushed. Try to strike a common middle ground between being overly enthusiastic and cautious. As a rule, Search Committee members should be in listening mode except when it comes to describing situations the new director will face. This is good advice to pass on to staff members as well.

It may be possible to schedule everything in a single day, but chances are, everyone—especially the candidate—will leave feeling exhausted. Two days will provide more opportunities to accommodate everyone's schedules and allow time for both the candidate and the Search Committee to "sleep on it." It's very important that the candidate have time to ask questions of the Search Committee and staff members. The schedule should include opportunities to meet with all key players, including, but not limited to, the following:

- the Search Committee, board chair, Executive Committee, and other board members, such as committee chairs
- senior staff members, such as department heads and chief curators
- key departments, such as interpretation/public programs
- tours of the museum campus, as well as off-site locations
- introductions to leaders of institutions with collaborative programs
- social gatherings—large meet-and-greet parties and smaller meetings, perhaps over meals, that allow for more in-depth conversation

Use judgment about which are best scheduled as individual meetings and which would be most effective as group meetings, and be flexible about accommodating the schedules of those involved. Also, consider the tone—formal meetings versus informal gatherings—allowing plenty of time for meaningful conversations. And remember that every aspect of the candidate's visit—from the time they're picked up at the airport or met at their hotel to the time they return home—is an opportunity for both parties to learn more.

Case in point: The eight members of the Search Committee at one museum divided their interview questions according to their areas of expertise. The incoming chair asked questions about long-range planning and management; the docent chair posed questions about education. After spending about two hours discussing these questions, a staff member took the candidate to the gift shop for fifteen minutes, giving the committee a chance to have a brief discussion about other areas they wanted to address or issues they needed to delve into further. They brought the candidate back, asked their questions, and then gave the candidate an opportunity to pose questions.

In general, the schedule should be full but not grueling. Candidates often appreciate a few hours to reflect on their introductions and do a little exploring on their own. Neighborhoods, shops, homes, and schools are all part of the equation for candidates. Some may request introductions to realtors to get a sense of market values, which may factor into their decision-making.

CHECK REFERENCES

Template 10: Reference Check

Once the Search Committee has selected its top candidate (or candidates), checking references may seem like a formality, but it is not. In fact, this single step can make the difference between the right and the wrong choice. At this point in the search process, there is a sense of relief and anticipation, and everyone wants the reference checks to confirm that the top candidates are all they say they are. But if they're not, it is far better to find out at this stage than six months into the tenure of the wrong candidate.

Template 10: Reference Check helps to clarify unanswered questions—gaps in dates between positions, reassignments within the same organization, or details of specific responsibilities listed on the resume. Use this document as a guide for your conversations. By giving each caller a link to the document, they can make notes directly on it, and the administrator can distribute their findings to the rest of the committee. By this time in the process, the pool has been narrowed down to just a few final candidates. For consistency, it is best if the same person does all of the reference checks. If that is not possible, this template will ensure that everyone asks the same questions and gets the same information.

TEMPLATE 10: REFERENCE CHECK

Please complete this form for each reference call for each candidate, and return it to the administrator by [date].

Name of candidate:

Name of reference:
Title:
Email:
Phone:

Name of caller:
Date:

Thank you for making the time to talk with me. [Name] is a candidate for director of {[Museum Name]}.

Provide a brief overview of the museum and a summary of the job description.

How long have you know this person?

What was the nature of your relationship? In what capacity do you know him/her?

What three to five adjectives would you use to describe [him/her]?

How would you characterize [his/her] relationship with the staff? Can you share an anecdote illustrating this?

How would you characterize [his/her] relationship with the board? Can you share an anecdote illustrating this?

How would you characterize [his/her] relationship with the community? Can you share an anecdote illustrating this?

How does [he/she] respond in a crisis? Can you share an anecdote illustrating this?

How effective is [he/she] in moving a group to action? Can you share an anecdote illustrating this?

What are [his/her] three greatest strengths or assets?

1.

2.

3.

What are [his/her] three most serious weaknesses or liabilities?

1.

2.

3.

I'd like to clarify the following dates, positions, and other information listed on the resume:

Although candidates have shared the names of references, it is a courtesy to let them know when you will be conducting reference checks so they can let their colleagues know to expect a call from your museum. Offer assurance that all inquiries will be treated with the utmost confidentiality, and be sure to get clarity on the issue of talking to the candidate's current employer. If he or she is openly searching for a new position, this usually doesn't present a problem. Otherwise, an inquiry could seriously jeopardize his or her current position.

Brian O'Connell says that when he receives reference calls, "With very few exceptions, I am appalled at how cursory the review is. As a consequence, I rarely have to be as candid as I would be if the questioning were sharp. This tells me that most people have made up their minds, but still want to go through the steps of clearance without having their decision shaken."[4]

People are all too eager to speak positively about former colleagues and staff members. It takes special skills to ask the right questions and get useful information, but many board members have had little experience checking candidates' references. Ideally, every board will include someone with a background in human resources. If yours does not, you may want to hire someone to do the reference checks as a separate piece of consulting or find a friend of the board who is willing to do some pro bono work for the museum. Many law firms have human resources departments with attorneys who might serve as consultants. If there's an attorney on your board, ask whether one of his or her colleagues could help in this way.

How can the Search Committee make the most of reference checks when legal counsel usually advises organizations to provide only minimal amounts of information on current or former employees? Verification of position, dates of employment, and corroboration of information on the resume are not very useful to a committee in the final stages of its decision-making process. What is needed is firsthand information from people who have worked with and for the candidates.

A human resources officer recommends talking to people who may not be so aware of liability issues, making them as comfortable as possible. If the tone is more of a conversation than an interview, people will often let down their guard and share their honest reactions. Ask for personal stories or anecdotes that will paint a picture of the candidate. Point out that everyone has strengths and weaknesses; strength in one organization might be a weakness in another and vice versa. Ask what professional skills or personal qualities the candidate might need to develop if he or she is hired. Request details about challenging situations the candidate mentioned in his or her interview.

It is foolhardy to rely only on the names provided by the candidate. It is wise to go beyond those references to other colleagues, so ask the candidates' permission to check other references in addition to those whose names they provide. Seek out individuals who know the candidate in a variety of ways, including those who have managed, worked with, and worked for the candidate. It's also a good idea to contact institutions the candidate has been associated with.

Case in point: In addition to checking references, it's wise to call the registrar's office at schools that awarded terminal degrees to confirm the information listed on the resume. Board members at one art museum were shocked to learn five years into their director's tenure that he had not earned the PhD he claimed to have. Any evidence of deception constitutes a red flag that must be diligently pursued.

Background Checks

Increasingly, boards are choosing to take the added precaution of doing a background check, which involves contracting an outside company licensed to perform this service. Academic records, college and graduate school degrees, publications, professional licenses, employment history, credit reports, driving records, criminal and civil court records, and private investigations can all be checked and verified. The fees for each vary, so the Search Committee can choose those reports it wants to run. The candidate must be informed and give their permission to conduct a background check. The museum, in turn, must enter into an agreement with the background check company giving it permission to act on the museum's behalf and informing the museum of its legal responsibilities as a receiver of confidential information. The costs for reference checks are typically borne by the museum, even when working with a search firm.

CONDUCT A SECOND INTERVIEW

Assuming that the reference checks on your top candidate or candidates are positive, you may want to invite them back for a second interview. This is a good opportunity to introduce the candidate(s) to a wider circle of internal and external audience members and see how they respond in social situations—an important factor since the director is on the front line with all of the museum's constituencies. A second interview is also a good opportunity for the candidate(s) to learn more about the museum and the community. If the candidate is married or in a long-term relationship, invite their spouse or partner as well, and be sure to plan activities for them.

Case in point: One museum handled the second interview as follows: The candidate spent the morning talking with senior staff members one-on-one, joined the Search Committee for lunch, and attended an evening reception. During the first hour of the reception, board members met the candidate and her spouse and visited informally. During the second hour, the museum invited community leaders and donors to hear the candidate make a fifteen-minute presentation. The rest of the evening was a social gathering and an opportunity for Search Committee members to seek out opinions of the candidate.

Another option for getting to know a final candidate better is for one or more members of the Search Committee to visit the museum where the candidate is presently employed. If he or she has already announced their departure, this visit can be scheduled with the candidate. If not, Search Committee members can learn a lot about the culture of a museum simply by experiencing it as regular visitors. Either way, seeing the candidate's current museum adds an important dimension to the decision-making process. If this is not possible, encourage final candidates to bring catalogs, photographs, articles, or other materials that would help the Search Committee to envision their current institution and their impact there.

SELECT THE NEW DIRECTOR

Once the references have been checked and the questions have been answered to everyone's satisfaction, the Search Committee must assess the candidates and recommend one or more final candidates to the board. These discussions must be open, frank, and constructive, with everyone having an opportunity to reflect on what they have learned, the needs of the museum, and the qualities each candidate brings to the position. This is not a conversation that can be rushed. Dissenters should feel that their perspectives have been given a fair and thoughtful hearing.

Once the Search Committee has agreed on the top candidate(s), they are brought to the board for the final decision. It is common for the committee to state pros and cons of each and leave it to the full board to select their top choice or to ratify the work of the committee. Ultimately, the appointment of a new director is the responsibility of the entire board, whether affirming the recommendation of a single candidate or choosing between two or more top candidates.

EXTEND AN OFFER

Once the board has made this vitally important decision, the Search Committee chair will offer the position to the finalist. Extending the offer and receiving a response may take several days. Only after the top candidate has accepted its offer should the committee contact the other finalists, thanking them for their interest.

Although trust is an important ingredient in any new relationship, we recommend that the committee draft a letter of agreement or an employment contract outlining the terms to which the board and the director have agreed.

Here again, an attorney who deals with personnel issues will be a great help. If you don't have one on your board, contract with one to write an agreement or to review your draft. Each agreement must be tailored to the specific circumstances of the museum and the candidate, but the following key elements should be considered:

- *Title and description of responsibilities.* Parts of the job description can be incorporated into the agreement.
- *Terms of agreement.* Specify the starting date and clarify any interim work that will be done before the start of full-time permanent employment.
- *Compensation.* Include starting salary, salary scale, basic benefits, and any additional benefits, such as a company car, parking privileges, membership, or bonuses.
- *Performance goals for the first year.* The director and the board will mutually agree on these goals during the first quarter.
- *Guidelines for the director's performance review.* Note who will conduct the review, the schedule, and the criteria on which it will be based.
- *Renewal and termination provisions.* Include definitions and timing guidelines for both parties.
- *Other.* Include moving allowances, support services, or special equipment required to perform the job and standards governing the acceptance of outside work.

Once the candidate signs the letter or contract, a copy should be kept in the personnel files.

NOTES

1. The American Alliance of Museums Salary Survey, developed in conjunction with the six regional museum associations, can be found at http://www.aam-us.org/about-us/media-room/2017-salary-survey. In addition to the full survey, an Administrative Snapshot that includes director/CEO/president is available for a reduced fee.

2. Derwin Dubose, "The Nonprofit Sector Has a Ferguson Problem," *Nonprofit Quarterly*, December 5, 2014, accessed July 27, 2017, https://nonprofitquarterly.org/2014/12/05/the-nonprofit-sector-has-a-ferguson-problem/.

3. Jan Masaoka, executive director, Support Center for Nonprofit Management, interview by Sean Bailey in *Philanthropy Journal Online* (July 1997).

4. Brian O'Connell, *The Board Member's Book* (Washington, DC: The Foundation Center, 1985), 27.

4

The Transition Stage

It is the responsibility of the Search Committee and the board to not only to *recruit* but also to *retain* the executive director. Many boards, having hired a new director, are inclined to heave a sigh of relief and say, "Thank goodness that job is done!" But in many ways, the most important part of the executive search process is just beginning. Once trustees have made such a significant investment in recruiting the best candidate, they need to maximize the return on that investment with continuing contributions of attention, time, and energy. One nonprofit board consultant tells her clients that their job as board members is twofold: to hire the best person, and then to make that person successful. The first year is crucial; the new director's first weeks and months on the job will have a profound effect on his or her long-term success.

PLAN THE TRANSITION

Template 11: Transition Calendar

While the new director's move may happen relatively quickly, his or her transition will take time. **Template 11: Transition Calendar** uses a quarterly calendar format to help the board, Search Committee, and Transition Team work with the new director to make plans and monitor progress throughout the transition. This template helps the board answer these questions:

- How can we best support the new leader?
- Whose involvement and perspectives are needed?
- What types of formal meetings and informal gatherings will help build important relationships?
- When do the various activities best fit into the crucial transition year?

The **Transition Calendar** (figures 4.1–4.4) provides a list of suggested activities that are scheduled throughout the transition year. The first quarter focuses on announcing the appointment to internal and external stakeholders, beginning the orientation process, and planning and budgeting for the transition. In the second quarter, the emphasis shifts to team building, networking, and establishing a schedule for regular meetings and special functions that will help the director get to know the staff and the community. In the third quarter, the director and the Transition Task Force initiate steps to strengthen the team, assessing the museum's current situation and considering necessary changes, including transition coaching. The fourth quarter focuses on building for the future through a formal assessment of the director and the board. This calendar can be easily modified to include other activities planned by the Search Committee, the Transition Task Force, and the new director.

Since every museum is different, the director and the board will choose the schedule and activities that best fit the institution and its community. Using the online Help Manual, the administrator will adjust the calendar to the museum's timeline, starting during the month when the Search Committee finalizes the agreement with the new director. The calendar assumes that the new leader will start one month after an agreement is reached, but individual circumstances may dictate a longer period. If the new director is not coming for two or more months, the museum may offer to pay for a short visit. This helps build momentum and lets the new director start thinking about his or her priorities before actually joining the staff. It also provides time to look for housing, schools, and other aspects of settling into a new community.

Since the sequence and duration of steps may vary, they can be moved around, added, or deleted from the four quarters. Some steps will overlap or extend over several months. As would be expected, the number of transition tasks diminishes over the year, but it is critical to keep the tasks on the board's list of priorities.

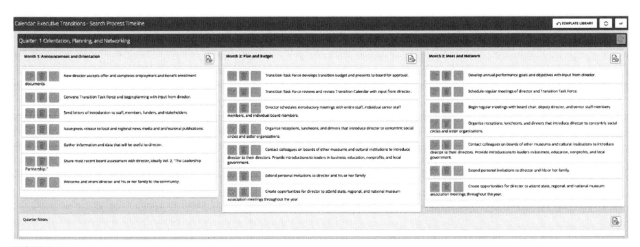

FIGURE 4.1
Transition Calendar: Quarter 1 (Courtesy of the Museum Trustee Association)

FIGURE 4.2
Transition Calendar: Quarter 2 (Courtesy of the Museum Trustee Association)

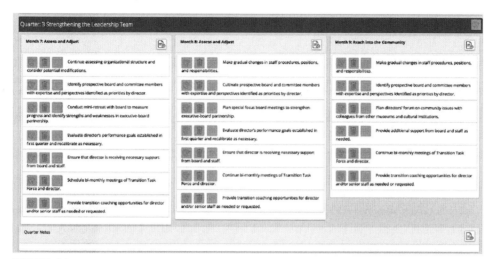

FIGURE 4.3

Transition Calendar: Quarter 3 (Courtesy of the Museum Trustee Association)

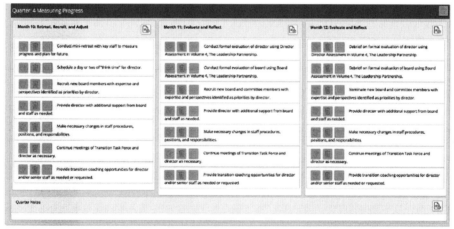

FIGURE 4.4

Transition Calendar: Quarter 4 (Courtesy of the Museum Trustee Association)

Develop a Transition Budget

After outlining the many steps that will occur in the first year, develop a transition budget to support them. Consider the following:

- Receptions to introduce the new director to various constituencies
- Regular and occasional meetings, such as board and staff retreats
- Professional development opportunities, such as coaching, workshops, and conferences
- Capital expenses, such as updated computers or office furnishings

Don't forget to include human resources in the planning and budgeting process. Consider the support that can be provided by outside facilitators or transition coaches as well as board members and staff. Involving a broad spectrum of museum stakeholders and engaging in community and professional networks will involve line items in the budget, but it is money well spent. This initial investment will pay dividends that multiply over each year of the director's tenure.

FORM A TRANSITION TEAM

Appoint a Transition Task Force

It is normal for board members—especially those who have served on the Search Committee—to feel relieved once they've finally hired the director and to be eager to hand things off to the new leader. But if they disappear at this crucial time, the director may feel abandoned by the very people who chose him or her. An executive search consultant says, "The relationship of a new leader with the board in the first few weeks is a good predictor of the relationship over time."[1]

That's why it's crucial to encourage Search Committee members who have the time and energy to stay on through the transition period and invite new board members to join a Transition Task Force. Executive Committee members and committee and task force chairs can play a key role in facilitating the new director's transition. And this is the perfect time to increase staff involvement. Sometimes referred to as "onboarding," this stage of the transition involves working closely with the new director to come to a shared understanding of how staff and board leaders will work toward common goals. Setting a collective leadership agenda will also identify any gaps in the new director's experience or the museum's capacity—or both—and make plans to fill them. This is a win/win opportunity because it provides board and staff members and the new leader with an excellent way to get to know one another! We recommend that this group meet monthly for the first two quarters, and then less frequently, as circumstances dictate. The director needs a safe place to go for advice and feedback on the politics of the institution and the community, so be sure to choose people who have experience and wisdom; avoid anyone who may have an agenda or an ax to grind.

One director says he appreciated having a small group of people he could turn to for help in sorting through the initial rounds of introductions and mounds of information. This group helped present the big picture and provided a buffer from individuals who might have been inclined to build personal alliances during his first months in the position.

Assemble Orientation Materials

Whether a new director finds an empty desk or a room full of files, books, and reports, he or she will need to have ready access to essential information about the museum and its internal constituencies. This information will help make sense of the countless people the director will meet and the mountains of material he or she will absorb in the first days and weeks on the job. Enlist the help of staff in pulling together the items listed in appendix A and ask the new director whether there are other things that would be helpful.

Case in point: One new director tells of walking into his office on the first day of his new job. Sitting down at his desk, he pulled open the drawers and found them empty. He proceeded to open every file drawer in the office and didn't find a single piece of paper from his predecessor's twenty-plus years at the museum. Now that's starting with a clean slate!

Involve the Director

A variety of perspectives are just as important to a successful transition as comprehensive information about the museum. Be sure to involve the new director in the transition planning process. To make the most of the director's involvement, the board should assume an inquiry mode rather than an advocacy mode. While trustees may know the museum and the community far better than the new director, advice is always more welcome from those who ask questions than from those who dictate a position. So ask the new director:

- What will be your entry strategy with the staff? With the board? With the community?
- How can we support you in each case?
- What would you like to do on your first day in the museum? In your first week? In your first month?

One new director identified three major areas that she needed to focus on when she first arrived:

1. *Building relationships.* Her greatest immediate need was for help in establishing relationships with staff, board, and community members.
2. *Budgeting.* Recent financial reports helped her to begin thinking about the business management aspects of leadership.
3. *Programming.* Descriptions of recent and upcoming programs gave her a sense of how the museum had been serving its community.

Once the director has a clear picture of relationships, resources, and programs, he or she should meet with the Personnel Committee or Executive Committee to discuss the strategic priorities for the first year and develop measurable goals and objectives. It is absolutely essential that these expectations be developed jointly and expressed in writing long before the director's annual assessment. Having clear, mutually agreed-upon standards by which his or her success will be measured will ensure that the first-year assessment is objective and constructive.

INTRODUCE THE DIRECTOR

Welcome the Director to the Community

High on the list of transition priorities is helping the new director and his or her family to get settled in your community. If the family feels comfortable and connected at home, the director will be better able to focus his or her energies on the job. There are many important ways the board can help. Learn everything you can about family members, their interests, and their needs, and then consider the following:

- Give the new director's family a tour of different neighborhoods, preferably by board or staff members who live in each area.
- If the director has children, introduce the family to different schools and to other children their age who share the same interests in sports and other extracurricular activities.
- Ask board and staff members to pick their favorite restaurants, and make a list with the name of the person who made each suggestion. This list will not only provide good dining tips but also serve as a conversation starter as the director gets to know the board and staff.
- Give the new director and his or her family a subscription to the monthly city magazine and/or arts publication.
- Consult with human resources departments of firms in your community. How do they help to relocate executives and their families and aid them in becoming acclimated to the area? Might they offer some pro bono assistance? And if they do, consider a complimentary membership to recognize their contribution.
- Ask board and staff members to extend personal invitations to the new director and his or her family to help them get to know what the community has to offer.

Case in point: One director tells the story of being invited to go trout fishing by a member of the Executive Committee at his favorite stream. Years later, the director remembered this simple experience as a confirmation of the rightness of his decision to come to that community. Another director who is a single parent always appreciated a board member's invitation to dinner. It was there that he met her thirteen-year-old daughter, who became the family's favorite babysitter until she went off to college.

Make Introductions and Extend Invitations

Think carefully about the process of inviting people into the community and the museum—not only the candidate but also his or her spouse or partner and other family members. What is the most gracious way to introduce them to the museum family? With whom would they and their family share common interests? What is the most appropriate way to introduce them to the business community? To funders? To colleagues at sister institutions? Board members are generally included in these early introductions, but they are not the only people the new director needs to meet. Remember to include staff and community members.

Introductions are especially critical if the director comes from out of town—and new museum directors often do. People who have lived in a community for many years may not realize how dependent the newcomer is on locals to help make that initial set of contacts. Organize receptions, lunches, and dinners that enable the new leader to meet concentric social circles: staff and board members, then major donors, then the general membership, and finally the community at large. The wider the circles get, the more help the new director needs in making connections.

These ideas can be incorporated into a transition plan:

- Send a press release to local and regional newspapers, as well as to professional publications.
- Feature the new director on the museum's website, perhaps in an interview format.
- Write letters to stakeholders announcing the new director's starting date, describing his or her background, and the person to call with questions until he or she arrives. Tailor these letters to what each individual or group will want to know about the new leader.
- Schedule opportunities for the director to get to know board members in relaxed social settings.

Facilitate Professional Networking

One of the board's most valuable contributions is to open doors for the new leader, providing access to social and business circles. The transition plan should include a formal strategy for introducing the director to key stakeholders in the community. The board has had a chance to meet the director and begin building relationships during the interview process. Now the director needs to meet many other groups and individuals to be successful operating in external circles. One director said that board introductions served as an institutional "seal of approval" that made him feel that he could speak for the museum.

Board members' connections will yield a list of people to include from various segments of the community, such as public and private education, higher education, foundations, business, civic groups, and local government. Networking through these individuals will help the new leader meet people who aren't on the usual lists. If, for example, the museum has a satellite facility or a community outreach program, the new director may want to meet some of the residents of the neighborhood. Offer to do whatever is necessary to make these connections.

BEGIN BUILDING RELATIONSHIPS

The Board Chair

One of the first priorities of the transition is to build a mutually supportive relationship between the director and the board chair. The strength of the relationship depends in large measure on whether the director sees the chair as a close partner who will share the responsibilities of leadership or as a remote challenger who will judge his or her performance. The Search Committee or Transition Task Force can help build a firm foundation for this relationship by helping the chair and director to see each other as strategic allies that complement rather than compete with one another.

The following suggestions will help the committee or task force cultivate positive first encounters between the two leaders:

- Share information about their common interests and qualities. Have they traveled to some of the same countries? Do they both enjoy running? Do their alma maters enjoy a healthy rivalry? Discovering what they have in common will help to bridge their different perspectives and approaches as they start to work together. Talking through differences of opinion can also deepen their appreciation of one another.
- Schedule regular meetings at times when both are free from distractions. In the first months, before the director's calendar gets packed, create opportunities for them to know one another as colleagues.
- Encourage them to establish effective, convenient mechanisms for communicating with one another. Technology offers a growing number of options. If each person knows the other's preferences, routines, and time schedules, their expectations will be consistent, and they will be accessible when they are needed.
- Remember that people who would be uncomfortable stranded on a desert island together can make great leadership partners. With mutual appreciation, different strengths can be seen as assets that complement one another.

The Board

While the Search Committee has a head start on getting to know the director, the full board should be eager to start forging connections too. After initial introductions to the full board, create opportunities for the director to meet with small groups such as committees or task forces. Also, suggest that individual board members make themselves available to talk with the new director one-on-one. Getting to know trustees as people often helps directors to appreciate the unique perspectives and contributions (monetary and otherwise) that each board member can make. This interaction will emphasize the usefulness of the board and build a mutually supportive partnership.

Case in point: One new director carved out time to sit down for two hours with each board member in her first few months on the job. Understanding that everyone wanted a chance to tell her their vision before she told them hers, she started by asking them questions such as "Why did you agree to serve on the board? What do you most love about the museum? What are its strengths and weaknesses?" She saved her notes from these conversations, planning to revisit them in a year or two. After spending this time getting to know board members as individuals, she knew she had their backing from the outset.

Once relationships are established, board members can be a sounding board for the new director, a safe place to go for advice and recommendations. Supporting a new director often means striking a delicate balance between providing assistance and giving the new leader time and space to figure things out. When asked about the most valuable support she got from her board during her first six months on the job, a director said, "They were there when I needed them, but they left me alone, respecting the time I needed to get my balance."

The new director needs to have a role in shaping a board that provides adequate support for the leadership partnership. The Governance Committee should initiate a conversation with the director about what kinds of support he or she would like in key areas such as finance, fundraising, investments, and legal issues. If there are no current board members with expertise in these areas, make it a priority to recruit them for the next board class. In the same way that the Search Committee considered the museum's stage in its institutional life cycle (see appendix C), it should consider board composition. A board needs to keep pace with the institution it leads. As CompassPoint's longitudinal study of nonprofit executive directors pointed out, "The composition of a board that has supported a long-time executive may well be different from the board that will be needed to recruit and hire a new leader."[2] For a thorough approach to board recruitment, see *Building Museum Boards*, volume 1 in the *Templates for Trustees* series.

The Staff

To help the new leader get off on the right foot with staff members, it is important to acknowledge that both the staff and the director are probably a little nervous. Even before making personal introductions, give the staff a little background on the director's leadership qualities and give the director a sense of the key staff players, their experience, and perspectives. Asked to identify the greatest sources of training and support in their work as executive directors, respondents to the CompassPoint survey chose their management team and colleagues first.[3]

The Search Committee or Transition Task Force can facilitate this kind of support by encouraging individual meetings with staff leaders early in the transition period. Encourage division or department heads to build a mutually rewarding relationship with their new leader by asking them to think about the following questions:

- What do I most need to know about the director and his or her management style?
- What does he or she most need to know about my department and me?
- What kind of working relationship would I like to have with the director?
- What can I do to create that relationship?

Meetings with the deputy (or associate or assistant) director are especially important. The job descriptions for these positions may reflect or complement the former director's strengths and weaknesses. With a new director, the deputy director's role is likely to change, creating the potential for both discomfort and exciting new possibilities. The Search Committee or Transition Task Force can help the deputy director to see the opportunities in a redefinition of responsibilities while helping the director to appreciate the value of the deputy's past contributions and exploring the best ways to use his or her talents and experience in the future.

If it is necessary to make changes, consider not only the deputy director but also other staff members who are impacted by the deputy's previous roles and responsibilities. In larger museums, the deputy director may be the primary contact for many staff members, so the change should be gradual and responsibilities clearly defined. Anxiety will generally diminish with time if the board, director, deputy, and staff simply affirm one another's feelings by saying, "This is difficult, isn't it? But after six months of working together, we'll have the situation ironed out." A simple statement like this can go a long way toward increasing comfort levels and building support for change.

After meeting with the deputy director and the senior management team, the director will want to get to know the rest of the staff. Depending on the staff size, he or she may want to meet with each department or have short, one-on-one meetings with each staff member.

Case in point: One director met with thirty employees during his first couple of months on the job. He said to each person, "I have your position description, but I'd like you to tell me what you do and how I could help you to do it better." These meetings lasted from thirty to sixty minutes, and they laid the foundation for good working relationships with the entire staff. In larger museums, the new director can make it a point to schedule meetings with each department.

Professional Peers

Another important source of training and support for executive directors of nonprofits is their peer network. The transition plan should include opportunities for the director to meet directors at other museums and cultural institutions soon after he or she arrives. Board members can talk with colleagues on the boards of other institutions to arrange these introductions. After the initial meetings, build on these peer relationships through opportunities to explore common concerns or shared projects. Invite other directors to forums on community issues, perhaps hosting the first one at your museum. Send the director to state, regional, and national museum association meetings to connect with colleagues. Include the dates for these meetings on the transition calendar.

Case in point: One new art museum director found that the hearings for major state grants provided an excellent forum for meeting colleagues. Through those connections, she began participating in the county cultural alliance, where she met leaders of performing arts and arts education organizations.

CONSIDER A TRANSITION COACH

Some new directors choose to retain a transition coach during their first year on the job. A seasoned director moving from a museum of comparable size may not need this kind of support. But a younger director, a director moving from a middle-management position, or a director coming from a small museum to a larger institution might find it invaluable to have a coach who can share his or her experience and perspective. Because executive transitions often lead to organizational transitions, a transition coach can also serve the staff by establishing a forum for communication between the director and the senior management team. If the new director has a different management style from the previous director, senior staff and middle managers may need help adjusting to the new working climate. A new director may also impact the dynamics of the executive/board relationship, and a coach can help here too, keeping an eye on the 40,000-foot view of the institution at large.

Case in point: A new director hired a transition coach because soon after she arrived on the job, she observed that while the senior managers were all successful individuals, they weren't functioning as a team. Within two months, the coach had held confidential interviews with each senior staff member about their hopes and concerns for the transition. She helped the director get to know staff members and find a productive working relationship with each of them. She also shared insights about the director, serving as a neutral counselor for the management team. She led them all in a daylong retreat, bringing in warmth and humor as they shared their goals, took personality tests, and talked about honoring the differences they each contribute to the strength of the management team.

To find a consultant who specializes in transition coaching, contact CompassPoint (www.compasspoint.org/coaching) or the Center for Nonprofit Management (https://cnmsocal.org/executive-coaching/executive-coaching/) or ask staff and board members for recommendations. Once you narrow down your search, it's vitally important to conduct interviews in order to find the right chemistry between the new director and the coach.

Coaches typically work with their clients anywhere from six months to a year, sometimes beginning with face-to-face meetings that evolve to videoconferences or phone consultations. Often the frequency of meetings is greater at the beginning of the new director's tenure—perhaps shifting from biweekly to monthly.

Some coaches charge a flat fee, some offer a menu of services, and some bill on an hourly basis. The cost can range from a few thousand dollars to $20,000, depending on the services provided. Even if your transition budget allows only for hiring a consultant to do some personality testing and conduct a half-day retreat to help staff appreciate their individual differences and contributions, it will be time and money well spent. Smaller museums that have not hired a search firm will find the services of a transition coach to be especially valuable in making the most of this pivotal moment in the museum's life cycle.

Case in point: One new first-time director was so pleased with the support she received from her coach that she decided to extend the contract to cover all senior managers. The board was pleased that she found the coaching productive and approved the additional funding. One of the services the coach provided was using a common personality profiling tool that helped to build communication within the senior management team. That experience was so successful that managers asked for funding and training so that they could do the same work in their departments and use the tools with new hires. In the end, every staff member benefited from the expertise of the coach.

Mentors for Understanding Museum Culture

New directors from the for-profit world or other cultural nonprofits may need another type of support: under-standing the specific issues around leading a museum. "We don't want [new directors from outside of museums] to start thinking like everyone else in the museum field," said Philip Nowlen, director of a program for new directors formerly offered by the Getty Leadership Institute, "but they do need to understand why everyone around the table may be shocked when they suggest an approach that worked in their previous position but has never been thought of in the museum."[4] Consider enlisting an experienced (perhaps retired) museum professional to serve as a mentor to the new director, someone who can introduce them to what they need to know about the history, values, and culture of museums. State or regional museum associations may be able to offer suggestions or provide other orientations to the profession.

PROVIDE TIME FOR REFLECTION

New executive directors often hit the ground running, and the pace quickly accelerates. The leader of an executive transition program warns, "Too many leaders are fighting fires from day one, and they miss a critical window to understand and assess the organization and build strong relationships. As a result, they get off to a limping start and could end up playing catch-up for years."[5] Though everyone—director, board, and staff—is anxious to get moving, it is important to build in time for reflection throughout the transition year. One of the factors in director burnout is that directors constantly have to attend to simultaneous and often conflicting needs. This leaves "little time for reflection and even less room for making mistakes."[6] Without reflection, mistakes are far more likely to occur.

Consider adding a few days of "think time" to the Transition Calendar. During the transition year, plan for mini-retreats where the director and senior management team can get away from the museum to engage in dia-logue about how things are going from everyone's perspective. It may be useful to enlist the help of an outside facilitator to lay a foundation of trust and collaboration. Create similar opportunities for the board to meet with the new director in a relaxed, retreat-like setting rather than in the boardroom.

Case in point: Opportunities for reflection can occur at any time during the executive transition cycle. One director gave two months' notice to his former employer before joining the staff at his new museum. During that period, the board invited him to attend its annual long-range planning retreat in a setting away from the museum. Since he had not yet assumed responsibility for leadership and everyone was on neutral territory, both arms of the leadership partnership were able to exchange ideas freely in a relaxed and open environment.

As the director settles in, it is important to take time out to discuss progress as well as challenges and frustrations. Midway through the transition year, revisit the director's performance goals and recalibrate them if necessary.

BUILD FOR THE FUTURE

During the second half of the transition year, the challenges for new directors shift from getting oriented and ac-quainted to working together and building for the future. A director who has been on the job for five months said, "My focus now is shifting to programmatic issues. In order for me to start making decisions about the next steps we're going to take, it is critical that we build enthusiasm for the new ideas that are being developed." By support-ing these budding visions and plans, the board can help to ensure that internal and external audiences are buying into the new vision of the institution.

Director Assessment

During the first quarter, the director and the board agreed on a clear set of goals and performance standards for the first year (see "Involve the Director," pages 56–57). These standards should be stated in clear and measurable terms so they can be evaluated and, if necessary, recalibrated throughout the transition year. They will be the basis for the director's first annual review at the end of the year. Human resources professionals characterize goals as SMART if they are:

- Specific
- Measurable
- Achievable
- Relevant
- Time-based

It is also important to include both performance goals, around the responsibilities of the position, and professional development goals, which revolve around learning.

In addition to monitoring the director's performance, the board should monitor his or her job satisfaction regularly using formal and informal means. *Daring to Lead* recommends that "board leadership should regularly consider not only the performance of their executives, but their levels of fatigue, stress, and frustration."[7] Never is this more important than during the first year. This is a time when the director's learning curve is so steep that he or she may need additional support. It is also a time when new systems are being put in place, and there is real potential to change things that may not be supporting the new leader. It is the board's responsibility to create a climate that allows the director to be effective.

Asking the new director to talk about the board and staff is a delicate issue. If the board takes offense at the director's comments, he or she may not feel safe speaking openly in the future. We recommend that a transition coach or a member of the Search Committee who is not on the board talk with the new director about the effectiveness of the support he or she receives and report to the Executive Committee, the Governance Committee, or the full board.

Suggested questions include:

1. How would you rate the support you're getting in each of the following areas?
   - Fundraising
   - Public relations and community relations
   - Strategic planning
   - Financial management
   - Human resources
   - Legal issues
   - Personnel issues
2. What additional support would you like to have from the board?
3. How could you better support the board?
4. What additional support would you like to have from the staff?
5. How could you better support the staff?
6. How well does the organizational structure support the museum's mission and strategic priorities?
7. How would you rate your stress level?
8. How comfortable are you with the museum's financial picture?
9. What is your biggest challenge in each of the following areas?
   - Human resources
   - Financial resources
   - Physical resources
   - Strategic alliances

It is important to realize that executive transition often brings organizational transition, as staff members re-evaluate their own roles. This is a normal, natural process, not necessarily a reflection on the Search Committee's choice or the new director's leadership. In the same way, a certain amount of transition on the board is normal and healthy. Some trustees may decide to leave with an outgoing leader. If they do, this is the right decision for them as individuals and for the institution. The spaces they leave will create opportunities to build a new board that is well suited to the challenges of new leadership.

Board Assessment

Because of its crucial role in an effective executive transition, the board may realize that an assessment of its own strengths and weaknesses could be especially fruitful at this time. If your board has used *The Leadership Partnership*, volume 2 in the Museum Trustee Association's *Templates for Trustees*, share the results of the Board Assessment (Template 2) with the incoming director. This overview will help him or her to get to know the board better, supplementing personal introductions and providing an unbiased view of board leadership. If you have not used the Board Assessment template, the end of the transition year presents an excellent opportunity to do so. In the interest of supporting the new leader, board members may be more inclined to examine governance patterns and to make changes if needed.

Whatever tools your board chooses, the transition year is the perfect opportunity to view assessment as an essential leadership skill that adds to the vitality of both board and staff leadership. With clear, mutually agreed-upon goals, the board will be able to measure—and celebrate—its success in selecting the right new director and the director's effectiveness in his or her new position.

NOTES

1. Lisa Walsh, Libbie Landles-Cobb, and Leah Karlins, "Boosting Nonprofit Board Performance Where It Counts," *Stanford Social Innovation Review*, July 16, 2014, accessed July 27, 2017, https://ssir.org/articles/entry/boosting_nonprofit_board_performance_where_it_counts.

2. Jeanne Peters and Timothy Wolfred, *Daring to Lead: Nonprofit Executive Directors and Their Work Experience* (San Francisco, CA: CompassPoint Nonprofit Services, 2001), 15.

3. Ibid., 32.

4. Philip Nowlen, telephone conversation with Daryl Fischer, February 2003.

5. Walsh, Landles-Cobb, and Karlins, "Boosting Nonprofit Board Performance Where It Counts."

6. Marjorie Schwarzer, "Turnover at the Top: Are Directors Burning Out?" *Museum News* 81, no. 3 (May/June 2002): 46.

7. Peters and Wolfred, *Daring to Lead*, 32.

Resource Guide for *Executive Transitions*

PUBLICATIONS

Abruzzo, James. "Selecting the Ideal Museum Director." DHR International, December 2013. Accessed July 26, 2017. http://www.dhrinternational.com/insights/selecting-ideal-museum-director/.

Adams, Tom. *The Nonprofit Leadership Transition and Development Guide: Proven Paths for Leaders and Organizations.* Hoboken, NJ: Jossey-Bass/John Wiley, 2017.

Allison, Michael. "Into the Fire: Boards and Executive Transitions." *Nonprofit Management and Leadership* 12, no. 4 (June 2002): 341–51. doi:10.1002/nml.12402.

American Alliance of Museums. *2017 National Museum Salary Survey.* Washington, DC: American Alliance of Museums, 2017.

Association of Art Museum Directors. *2017 Salary Survey.* New York: Association of Art Museum Directors, 2017.

Bailey-Bryant, Joy. "We're Not That Hard to Find: Hiring Diverse Museum Staff," *Museum* 96, no. 1 (January/February 2017): 27–29.

Bell, Jean, Paola Cubías, and Byron Johnson. *Will We Get There Hire by Hire? Reflections on Executive Leadership and Transition Data Over 15 Years.* Oakland, CA: CompassPoint, 2017. Accessed July 26, 2017. https://www.compasspoint.org/sites/default/files/documents/Hire_by_Hire_Report.pdf.

Bridges, William, and Susan Bridges. *Managing Transitions: Making the Most of Change,* 25th anniversary edition. Boston, MA: Da Capo Press, 2017.

CompassPoint. "Revisiting Executive Transitions: Who Leads and How?" Accessed July 26, 2017. https://www.compasspoint.org/revisiting-executive-transitions-who-leads-and-how.

Cornelius, Maria, Rick Moyers, and Jeanne Bell. *Daring to Lead 2011: A National Study of Nonprofit Executive Leadership.* Oakland, CA: CompassPoint and Meyers Foundation, 2011. Accessed July 26, 2017. http://daringtolead.org/wp-content/uploads/Daring-to-Lead-2011-Main-Report-online.pdf.

Ferrin, Richard W. *The Time Between: A Report of Museum Interim Executive Leadership Patterns.* Knoxville, TN: The Wakefield Connection, 2002.

Merritt, Elizabeth. "Taking the Bias Out of Hiring," *Museum* 96, no. 1 (January/February 2017): 21–24.

O'Connell, Brian. *The Board Member's Book.* New York, NY: Foundation Center, 2003.

Perry, Elissa, and Jamie Schenker. "Multiple Styles of Leadership: Increasing the Participation of People of Color in the Leadership of the Nonprofit Sector." Leadership Learning Community, 2005. Accessed July 26, 2017. http://leadershiplearning.org/system/files/Final_AECF_Web.pdf.

Peters, Jeanne, and Timothy Wolfred. *Daring to Lead: Nonprofit Executive Directors and Their Work Experience.* Oakland, CA: CompassPoint Nonprofit Services, 2001.

Schwarzer, Marjorie. "Turnover at the Top: Are Directors Burning Out?" *Museum News* 81, no. 3 (May/June 2002): 42–49, 67–69.

Stevens, Susan Kenny, PhD. *Nonprofit Lifecycles: Stage Based Wisdom for Capacity Building,* 2nd edition. Long Lake, MN: Stagewise Enterprises, Inc., 2002.

Tebbe, Don. *Chief Executive Transitions: How to Hire and Support a Nonprofit CEO.* Washington, DC: BoardSource, 2008.

Thomas-Breitfeld, Sean, and Frances Kunreuther. "Race to Lead: Confronting the Nonprofit Racial Leadership Gap." Building Movement Project, 2017. Accessed July 26, 2017. http://www.racetolead.org/.

W. K. Kellogg Foundation. "Racial Equity Resource Guide." Accessed July 26, 2017. http://www.racialequityresourceguide.org.

Walsh, Lisa, Libbie Landles-Cobb, and Leah Karlins. "Boosting Nonprofit Board Performance Where It Counts." *Stanford Social Innovation Review,* July 16, 2014. Accessed July 26, 2017. https://ssir.org/articles/entry/boosting_nonprofit_board_performance_where_it_counts.

Welling, Curtis R., and John H. Vogel Jr. "A Practical (and Possibly Provocative) Approach to Leadership Transitions." *Nonprofit Quarterly*, May 21, 2015. Accessed July 26, 2017. https://nonprofitquarterly.org/2015/05/21/a-practical-and-possibly-provocative-approach-to-leadership-transitions/#.

Wolfred, Tim. *Building Leaderful Organizations: Succession Planning for Nonprofits.* Baltimore, MD: Annie E. Casey Foundation, 2008. Accessed July 26, 2017. https://www.compasspoint.org/sites/default/files/documents/526_buildingleaderfulorganiza.pdf.

MUSEUM ASSOCIATION JOB POSTINGS

American Association for State and Local History. AASLH Career Center. http://jobs.aaslh.org/.

American Alliance of Museums. www.aam-us.org/resources/careers.

Association of African American Museums. www.blackmuseums.org/jobs.

Association of Art Museum Directors. www.aamd.org/museum-careers/current-opportunities.

Association of Children's Museums. www.childrensmuseums.org/members/resources/classifieds.

Association of Midwest Museums. www.midwestmuseums.org/jobs/.

Association of Science-Technology Centers. ASTC Job Bank. www.astc.org/job-bank/.

Association of Zoos and Aquariums. Career Center. www.aza.org/jobs.

Mid-Atlantic Association of Museums. Job Board. www.midatlanticmuseums.org/resources/jobs/.

Mountain-Plains Museum Association. Job Bank. https://www.mpma.net/Jobs.

New England Museum Association. NEMA Jobs. www.nemanet.org/resources/career-center/nema-jobs.

Southeastern Museums Conference. www.semcdirect.net.

Western Museums Association. Job Board. www.westmuse.org/job_board.

OTHER JOB POSTINGS

College Art Association. http://careercenter.collegeart.org/jobs.

Global Museum. www.globalmuseum.org.

Idealist. https://www.idealist.org/en/?sort=relevance&type=ALL.

Indeed.com. www.indeed.com.

Museum Employment Resource Center. www.museum-employment.com.

Museum Jobs. www.museumjobs.com.

Philanthropy News Digest. philanthropynewsdigest.org/jobs.

ORGANIZATIONS

Alliance for Nonprofit Management, 1732 1st Avenue, #28522, New York, NY 10128. Phone: 888-776-2434. Website: www .allianceonline.org.

American Alliance of Museums, 2451 Crystal Drive, Suite 1005, Arlington, VA 22202. Phone: 202-289-1818. Website: www .aam-us.org.

ArtTable, 1 E. 53rd St., New York, NY 10022. Phone: 212-343-1735. Website: http://www.arttable.org/.

Association of Executive Search and Leadership Consultants, 425 Fifth Avenue, 4th floor, New York, NY 10016. Phone: 212-398-9556. Website: www.aesc.org.

Boardnet USA, a service of The New York Council of Nonprofits, Inc., 272 Broadway, Albany, NY 12204. Phone: 800-515-5012. Website: boardnetusa.org.

BoardSource, 750 9th Street NW, Suite 650, Washington, DC 20001. Phone: 202-349-2580. Website: www.boardsource.org.

CompassPoint Nonprofit Services, 500 12th Street, Suite 320, Oakland, CA 94607. Phone: 510-318-3755. Website: www .compasspoint.org.

GuideStar Nonprofit Directory. Phone: 800-421-8656. Website: https://www.guidestar.org/NonprofitDirectory.aspx.

Management Center, 1920 L. St NW, Suite 775, Washington, DC 20036. Phone: 202-559-7475. Website: www .managementcenter.org/resources/.

Museum Trustee Association, 211 East Lombard Street, Suite 179, Baltimore, MD 21202. Phone: 410-402-0954. Website: www.museumtrustee.org.

National Council of Nonprofits, 1001 G Street NW, Suite 700 East, Washington, DC 20001. Phone: 202-962-0322. Website: www.councilofnonprofits.org.

Appendix A

Checklist of Materials for Interim Director and Incoming Director

INTERIM DIRECTOR

Organizational Information

- Bylaws
- Mission and vision statements
- Board minutes for last three years
- Corporate seal

Financial Information

- Form 990s
- Budgets and periodic financial statements
- Bank name, account numbers, and passwords
- Blank checks and authorized signers

Contacts, including name, phone number(s), email:

- Banker
- Investment representative
- Auditor
- Legal counsel

Human Resources Information

- Employee records and personnel contact information
- Board roster with contact information

Independent Contractors Information (including company, representative, contact info, and passwords)

- Security system
- Computer system

Insurance Information (for general liability and commercial umbrella policies)

- Company
- Policy number(s)
- Representative's contact information
- Broker's contact information

INCOMING DIRECTOR
The following lists include information that should be provided *in addition to* what has already been shared with the interim director.

Board

- Board roster with business affiliation and areas of expertise (consider including a photograph of each board member)
- Board minutes for the last year, including consent agendas
- Board committee structure
- Board manual
- Directors and Officers Liability Insurance, including company, policy number, and representative contact information

Staff and Volunteers

- Employee records
- I-9 forms for employment eligibility verification
- Staff roster, including photographs and brief biographies
- Staff organization chart
- Position descriptions
- Employee policies and procedures manual
- Health and dental insurance policies, including company, policy number, and representative contact information
- Life and long-term care insurance, including company, policy number, and representative contact information
- Unemployment, workers' compensation, and disability insurance, including company, policy number, and representative contact information
- Retirement plan, including company, policy number, and representative contact information
- Volunteer records
- Volunteer roster, including photographs
- Volunteer organization chart

Organizational and Financial Information

- Employer Identification Number (EIN)
- IRS Form 1023, Application for Exempt Status
- Copy of IRS letter granting 501(c)(3) status
- IRS Form 990, Return of Organization Exempt from Income Tax
- State or other Sales-Tax Exemption Certificate

- Current and prior year's budgets
- Annual reports for the last two to three years
- Two years of audit reports and management recommendation letters with auditor's contact information
- Vendor records
- Office and facility procedures

Strategy and Planning

- Strategic plan and periodic updates on progress

Fundraising

- Donor records
- Fundraising events, including descriptions, dates, and net revenues
- Grant proposals—awarded, denied, and in-progress
- For in-progress grant projects, include the funding source, contact person, beginning and end dates, and interim reports
- Funding documents from foundations, corporations, and government agencies

Program Information

- Program descriptions, including attendance statistics
- Audience evaluations conducted by staff and consultants
- Exhibition schedule
- Recent museum publications, such as exhibition catalogs, member newsletters, and program brochures

Appendix B

Ground Rules for Effective Meetings

To make the most of the many meetings that will be conducted throughout the executive search process, we recommend that the Search Committee chair review these guidelines with all committee members at the beginning of the groundwork stage.

1. **Encourage active participation.** All Search Committee members will participate actively in each phase of the search process. Each person has been invited to participate because of his or her unique perspective, so everyone's participation is essential and equally valuable. It is the chair's responsibility to make sure that each voice is heard.

2. **Keep discussions focused.** The discussions will stay focused on issues that are relevant to identifying the new leader. This means that there will be more time spent discussing the future than the past. If the discussion starts to get off track, it is the chair's responsibility to ask, "How will this information be useful to us in identifying the best candidate for the position?"

3. **Share information.** All relevant information will be shared with all members of the Search Committee. Sharing information is a way of empowering all members of the committee to serve effectively. It is the responsibility of each person to share all relevant information they know or hear, even if it doesn't support their views.

4. **Create a safe climate.** Make sure all members of the Search Committee feel that it is safe to disagree openly with one another. Speaking openly is critical at each stage of the process. To make the best decisions, Search Committee members need to gain an understanding of viewpoints that differ from their own.

5. **Discuss the undiscussable.** Sometimes the issues that are the hardest to bring up are the ones that most need to be aired. If Search Committee members believe that some issues are off limits, they will not be able to bring all issues to the table.

6. **Ask for examples.** Avoid generalities and challenge those who use them to be specific, providing concrete examples if possible. Citing directly observable behaviors allows others to form their own conclusions about each person's points.

7. **Be clear.** Clarify the meaning of unfamiliar or ambiguous words. Make sure that everyone in the group understands the meaning of all words and that all group members mean the same thing when they use a word.

8. **Explain your thinking.** Explaining the reasoning behind questions and statements helps people to interpret what others are saying correctly, reducing the chances of misunderstandings or erroneous assumptions. Encourage people to say, "I'm asking this because . . ." or "I mention this because . . ."

9. **Invite questions and comments.** After someone makes a statement, encourage others to comment by saying, "I understand X to be saying . . . Some of you may feel differently. I'd like to hear what you think, even if you disagree."

10. **Avoid taking positions.** Focus on goals rather than positions. Stating points in terms of positions can obscure goals that may be held in common. A goal is a positive way to meet a challenge—for example, "I think the next director should be able to understand the perspectives of underserved audiences." A position outlines a specific solution—for example, "I think we should hire a director who is a person of color."

11. **Respect one another.** It is easy to respect someone who holds a popular view, but respecting someone with divergent perspectives can be challenging. It is the responsibility of the facilitator to make sure that all members are treated with equal respect and cheap shots will not be tolerated. (See ground rule 4.)

12. **Come to consensus.** Although agreement is not always possible, consensus means that all Search Committee members can and will support the group's decisions. If even one member can't live with the group's decision, the facilitator must determine how the decision would need to be changed in order to achieve consensus. Reaching consensus takes more time than voting, but it pays off in terms of buy-in. "All those in favor, say 'aye'" assumes that silence means consent. To reach consensus, each person must state whether he or she consents.

Appendix C

Search Committee Retreat Activities

The following activities can help the Search Committee conduct a deeper exploration of the museum's current leadership issues and determine what experience and qualifications are needed in a new director. They are designed for use in a retreat setting after **Template 4: Institutional Audit** has been completed. Choose the activities that are most appropriate for the composition of the group and the time available, and ask the administrator to record the results.

STRENGTH/WEAKNESS ANALYSIS

This activity will answer the questions: What are the museum's greatest strengths, and how might they be grouped to create synergy? What are the museum's greatest weaknesses, and what do they have in common?

1. Create an unlabeled quadrant on a flip chart or whiteboard and distribute two different colors of Post-it notes to each participant.
2. Ask each person to write the museum's greatest strength on one color Post-it note and place it in the quadrant anywhere that makes sense. As committee members place their strengths with, adjacent to, or opposite others' strengths, a system of organization will emerge that reflects the Search Committee's strategic priorities. Which of these strengths will be most useful in the future? Are there any strengths that might lead to weaknesses? Individuals and institutions have a tendency to rely heavily on their strengths, which can create weaknesses in other areas. For example, a museum with a large endowment does not need to rely on revenues for support, but it can then become isolated from the community.
3. Next, ask each person to write the museum's most serious weakness on the other color of Post-it note, placing it wherever it seems to fit on the quadrant. Reflect on how the Post-its are organized. Are there any related strengths and weaknesses that are adjacent to one another? Are there any factors that are written on both colors of Post-its? Looking at the most serious weaknesses, are there any that hold potential for positive growth?

SWOT ANALYSIS

This activity builds on the previous analysis of internal strengths and weaknesses, which tends to be current, and adds external opportunities and threats, which may be future-oriented.

1. Create an unlabeled quadrant on a flip chart or whiteboard.
2. Label the upper-left quadrant *Strengths*; the upper-right, *Weaknesses*; the lower-left, *Opportunities*; and the lower-right, *Threats*. Draw a line in the middle with an upward-facing arrow pointing to *INTERNAL* and a downward-facing arrow pointing to *EXTERNAL*.

3. List the greatest strengths identified in the previous exercise in the upper-left quadrant. Then list the most serious weaknesses in the upper-right quadrant. Are there any related strengths and weaknesses? If so, what does this suggest about the professional skills and/or personal qualities needed in the new director?

4. List the greatest opportunities in the lower-left quadrant and the greatest threats in the lower-right. Many threats present corresponding opportunities to respond to changing conditions in ways that will make the organization stronger. Are there any related opportunities and threats? If so, what does this suggest about the professional skills and/or personal qualities needed in the new director?

To determine opportunities and threats, the Search Committee will need to extend its view beyond the museum walls, looking into the community and beyond. In the case of a museum that collects contemporary art, a nationally known archive of the writings of a Bauhaus master could be a strength on which to build. A new contemporary art museum that is opening in a neighboring city could be a threat to overcome.

TREND ANALYSIS

The following questions will help the Search Committee consider trends:

- What changes do we see in the environment? Rank them in terms of their potential to affect the museum.
- What are the critical issues this year? What will they be in three to five years?
- What opportunities do we have now that didn't exist last year?
- What new threats have emerged during the past year?
- What old threats continue to concern us?

The answers to these questions will help the Search Committee zero in on the qualities it seeks in the new leader. Try posing questions such as these:

- Do we need a change agent or a stabilizer at this stage of our institutional life cycle, someone to lead us in new directions or maintain the course?
- Do we need someone who is going to build new bridges in the community or someone who will maintain existing relationships?
- What interpersonal skills do we most need to move the institution forward: team building, inspiration, dedication, passion?
- What kind of vision will it take to turn the threats into opportunities?

INSTITUTIONAL LIFE CYCLE

A discussion of the institutional life cycle can help the Search Committee identify the kind of leadership the museum needs at this point in its evolution. The following life-cycle model by Susan Kenny Stevens includes seven stages, their characteristics, and their leadership styles.[1]

1. **Idea Stage**

   Characteristics: In this first stage, there is no formal organizational structure: primarily an idea or mandate to fill a societal, programmatic, or cultural gap. The idea operates with little or no budget and relies on volunteer effort and sweat equity.

Leadership style: The idea is often driven by a dominant, charismatic leader who lights the spark and cultivates the attitude that anything is possible. Founders are believable, action-oriented people with a commitment to a proposed purpose. In a museum, a founder may be an individual with a collection that will form the core of the museum's permanent collection or a group of passionate civic leaders with a vision to create a new community asset.

2. **Startup Stage**

   Characteristics: Energy and passion remain supreme in startups. The organization's legal status is established, and the board (often composed of constituents, friends, and supporters of the founder) is formally established. Although museums with collections or buildings often have higher fixed costs than other nonprofits, startups run on meager budgets.

   Leadership style: The startup requires a leader (paid staff, volunteer, or board chair) who is single-minded but adaptable and willing to take risks.

3. **Growth Stage**

   Characteristics: Mission and programs have taken hold, but the drive to provide services can exceed structural and resource capabilities. As organizations grow, they are challenged to find their "distinctive competence." The staff and volunteers that started the organization may struggle with change as specialists are hired. Founders often resist new directions, formalization of systems, and greater board oversight. The board assumes greater responsibility and understands its role, replacing hands-on work with committees and other more formal structures and reporting (including financial and program reporting). Salaries, benefits, equipment, and systems all require upgrading if the organization is to grow.

   Leadership style: This organization must be led by people who have the capacity to inspire and motivate others, create a plan but veer from it when necessary, and are comfortable with a very rapid pace of change.

4. **Maturity Stage**

   Characteristics: This is the stage that many functioning nonprofits, particularly museums, are in. The organization is well-established and operating smoothly. It enjoys a strong reputation and delivers relevant, high-quality service. The board has evolved into a policy-driven body that understands its role and does not micromanage, with clear tasks and term limits. Founders separate or evolve, resolving those tensions. Reliable, diverse, and ongoing funding sources are established. To stay fresh and vital, healthy organizations shift back and forth between Growth and Maturity, renewing programs and services.

   Leadership style: Executive leadership is often second or third generation from founders, so maintaining organizational culture can be a challenge. This stage requires experienced, competent management that sees the value of stability while seeking new directions.

5. **Decline Stage**

   Characteristics: As services become less relevant or exciting, attendance and revenue decline. The organization remains stuck, ignoring market needs and demands. An organization in decline has a rigid, inward focus more centered on staff and management than on constituent or audience. Funding may appear to be adequate for a time until investments and cash reserves are eroded. In museums, the collection often appears to be an attractive source of financial resources, triggering an ethical debate. The staff may be able to keep the board in the dark until new board members or staff sound the alarm. Outside consultants may be hired to assess the options for turnaround or termination.

   Leadership style: The successful leader at this stage takes responsibility rather than blames others or denies reality. If the organization is to move from Decline to Turnaround (rather than continuing into the Terminal stage), leaders must be capable of objective analysis, clear thinking, and initiating steps toward renewal. Too often, organizations in this stage fail to recognize the need for fresh leadership.

6. **Turnaround Stage**
   Characteristics: With declining public support, the organization is at a critical juncture that requires decisive action to reverse. The dramatic actions of a turnaround are often precipitated by crises and a serious financial situation. The period of decline may leave the organization with deteriorating facilities and flagging morale. It is often necessary to replace board or staff members and/or to eliminate staff positions.
   Leadership style: The turnaround leader is a gutsy, strong-willed manager with energy and faith in the organization, a clear sense of direction, and the ability to inspire confidence in others. The leader must be able to make quick short-term decisions but also be capable of long-term strategic thinking.

7. **Terminal Stage**
   Characteristics: Lacking will, purpose, or energy to continue to exist, the organization may technically be in business running marginalized operations and further depleting resources. It is necessary to close honorably and communicate termination plans to stakeholders and funders. In museums, it is ethically mandatory to find other public organizations to assume care of collections.
   Leadership style: There is generally only a skeleton staff in this stage, perhaps working without pay because they care about the organization and collections and want to see an orderly and responsible closing.

After reviewing these stages, have a discussion about where your museum fits. It may fall somewhere in between two stages, suggesting that the Search Committee should look for someone with the leadership styles of both stages.

NOTE

1. Susan Kenny Stevens, *Nonprofit Lifecycles: Stage Based Wisdom for Capacity Building*, 2nd edition (Long Lake, MN: Stagewise Enterprises, 2002), 26, 71–72.

About the Museum Trustee Association and the Authors

The Museum Trustee Association was formed as a committee of the American Association of Museums (now known as the American Alliance of Museums) in 1971. Time revealed that the differences of focus, responsibility, and interest between museum professionals and volunteer boards of trustees would be better served by a separate nonprofit organization. The Museum Trustee Association became a separate entity in 1986 and received its federal IRS 501(c)(3) status in 1991. Since then, MTA has been governed by an elected board of directors representing diverse regions of the United States, the Caribbean, Canada, and Mexico, a variety of museum disciplines and sizes, and wide-ranging areas of expertise in trusteeship. All are current or former museum trustees, and several are founders of MTA.

Daryl Fischer founded Musynergy Consulting in 1993 to provide strategic and interpretive planning, audience evaluation, and board development services to museums and other cultural nonprofits. In 2001 she coauthored the first edition of *Building Museum Boards*, followed by *The Leadership Partnership* (2002), *Executive Transitions* (2003), and *Strategic Thinking and Planning* (2004). Her service on numerous nonprofit boards including the Urban Institute for Contemporary Arts (Grand Rapids, Michigan), the Visitor Studies Association, and the Progressive Women's Alliance of the Lakeshore has given her a profound appreciation for the passion, energy, and expertise that board members bring to the organizations they serve. Her consulting practice has taught her that there is no one-size-fits-all formula for maximizing board effectiveness; however, authentic collaboration with staff and community members leads to a whole that is greater than the sum of the parts. Daryl has an MA from the University of Denver and a BA from Colorado College.

Laura B. Roberts is principal of Roberts Consulting, working with cultural nonprofit organizations on strategic planning, assessment, and organizational development. Laura was executive director of the New England Museum Association and the Boston Center for Adult Education. Previously, she was director of education at three history museums. She is the chair of the Central Square Theater in Cambridge, Massachusetts, and formerly chaired the boards of Tufts University Art Gallery, MassHumanities, and First Night Boston. She teaches museum and nonprofit management at Harvard University Extension, Bank Street College of Education, and Northeastern University. Laura holds an MBA from Boston University Questrom School of Business, an MA from the Cooperstown Graduate Program, and a BA from Harvard University.